DICTIONARY OF BRITISH
ANTIQUE SILVER

Elizabeth Felton as Cleopatra (detail),
by Benedetto Gennari, temp. Charles II,
showing silver two-handled drinking cup.

Dictionary of British Antique Silver

DOUGLAS ASH F.S.A.

Hippocrene Books, Inc. – New York

First published in the United States by
HIPPOCRENE BOOKS INC
171 Madison Avenue,
New York, N.Y. 10016
1972

ACKNOWLEDGEMENTS

The author wishes to thank Lady Muriel Martin and Mr B. W. Robinson, M.A., Keeper of the Department of Metalwork, Victoria and Albert Museum, London, who kindly read the proofs.

INTRODUCTION

Preaching to the converted is always an agreeable task, but it is more necessary to enlighten those who are interested in a subject but have little or no knowledge of it. That is the purpose of this book, which is presented in the form of a dictionary for ease of reference. Over the years, a number of sound and scholarly books on silver have been published and also several very bad ones. Even in the best, an enquiring layman often finds it laborious and discouraging to follow up separate entries on the same subject in an index and then correlate them, but here, all the requisite information will be found under the various headings. The widespread and increasing interest in old British and Irish silver among the English-speaking peoples has now rendered this method of presentation particularly desirable. In the following pages, while necessarily presupposing a reasonable standard of education, the author has endeavoured to bear in mind, without patronage, Rousseau's well-known recommendation to preceptors: 'Gentlemen, do yourselves the honour of coming down to the level of your pupils.'

This book is concerned with an extensive period beginning in the Anglo-Saxon era and ending in the early 19th century, but some readers may wonder why no attention has been paid to the numerous productions of the reign of Queen Victoria, which extended from 1837 to 1901. Much excellent domestic plate of the more modest sort was made during this long expanse of years, but the reason why there are no specific entries here relating to them is because there was no true Victorian style. Throughout most of the 19th century, following the waning of the Regency style, inspiration was generally drawn from the conceptions of previous stylistic phases. These were either reproduced more or less exactly, with admirable skill, or used in modified versions in which their origin was sometimes superficially disguised by contemporary accretions of inferior artistic merit. When Victorian designers strove to be original, the results were almost invariably unfortunate and it is not for nothing that the French refer to the Victorian age as *l'âge du mauvais goût*.

Throughout the period covered by this book there was, not unnaturally, a general affinity between the plate of England, Scotland and Ireland. But although the greater wealth and larger population of

England provided conditions which were conducive to a bigger volume of production, the craftsmanship of the silversmiths in England's sister nations in the British Isles was in no way inferior. The name of Ireland has not been included in the title of this book simply from a desire to keep it short, but the balance will be found to be redressed in the text by the inclusion, on equal terms, of the more important Irish centres among those of Scotland and England. Many, in all three countries, have been excluded, primarily owing to the paucity of surviving identifiable artefacts, which renders them comparatively unimportant. Personal experience and opinions are bound to enter into such a matter to some extent, but interested readers will find references to any neglected centres such as Lewes, Tain and Youghal in works mentioned in the Bibliography.

From ancient times, the British Isles have been rich in objects made of precious metal, and Celtic and English plate-workers developed something of an international reputation. In the 9th century, an Anglo-Saxon school of goldsmiths was working in Rome for the Holy See, and William the Conqueror's chaplain and chronicler, William of Poitiers, bore witness to the astonishment of the Norman invaders at the vessels of gold and silver in England in 1066. It is probable that no other country in the world can compare with England in the enthusiasm with which its inhabitants collected plate from the middle ages onward. Until the late 17th century, drinking vessels formed by far the most important single group. It must not be supposed, however, that our ancestors felt any attachment to their domestic plate on account of its antiquity; this is an attitude which has developed since the 19th century. They appreciated its beauty and enjoyed the prestige which its possession conferred upon them, but they also regarded it as a reserve of capital which could be realized if the necessity arose. The same unsentimental outlook ensured its destruction if fashions underwent a decided change, as from the Gothic to the renaissance, and much delightful medieval plate must have been melted in the early 16th century to be rewrought in the new style.

We read that at Cardinal Wolsey's palace of Hampton Court, on the occasion of a feast, 'there was a Cupbord made (for the tyme) in lengthe of the bredthe of the nether end of the same chamber of VI deskes highe, full of gilt plate very somptious & of the most newest facions and vppon the nether most deske garnysshed all w^t plate of clean gold hauyng II great Candylstykes of syluer & gylt most Curiously wrought . . . this Cupbord was barred in round abought that no man myght come nyghe it ffor there was none of the same plate occupied or sterred duryng this feast for ther was sufficient besides'. It is unfortunate that the 'candylstykes' in particular have not survived. Nearly all of this plate in the 'most newest facions' was almost certainly made from outmoded plate in the Gothic style which had been melted to furnish the raw material.

It is clear from the above account that the cardinal was displaying some of his investments for the admiration of his guests in accordance with contemporary practice, but in the second half of the 16th century, the remarkable position was reached that the use of plate was so widespread, that wealthy people considered that it no longer attracted a sufficiency of either respect or envy. While keeping their silver for its value, they accordingly turned their attention to expensive exotic objects which were easily broken, in order to demonstrate their affluence. 'It is a world to see in these our days', wrote William Harrison in 1587, 'wherein gold and silver most aboundeth, how that our gentility, as loathing those metals (because of the plenty) do now generally choose the Venice glasses, both for our wine and beer.' This particular snobbism was, however, destined to be comparatively short-lived. Emigrant glass-makers from Venice and Altare were assisting in the establishment of glass industries in western Europe and Queen Elizabeth I had already granted a twenty-year patent to Jacopo Verzelini in 1575 to make 'Venice glasses' in London. Production increased in the 17th century with a consequent growth of popularity and an eventual abatement of value and prestige. In any event, the piece of coxcombry mentioned by Harrison affected only the upper strata of society since the bulk of the population remained more impressed by solid worth than costly fragility, so that the national mania for plate-collecting suffered no diminution.

A record of 1635 bore witness to the large amounts of plate owned by 'every taverner' and went on to state that 'private householders in the citie, when they make a feast to entertane their friends, can furnish their cup boards with flagons, tankards, beere cups, wine bowls, some white, some parcel guilt, some guilt all over; some with covers, others without, of sundry shapes and qualities'.

This remained the situation until after the outbreak of the Civil War in 1642. When it was over, the bulk of England's vast treasure of silver had disappeared: melted down for conversion into coin for the payment of both contending armies.

After the restoration of the Monarchy in 1660, not only were vigorous steps taken to replace, in new styles, what had been destroyed, but an increased national demand was stimulated by Continental influence which entered the British Isles with the returning royalist exiles. Silversmithing activity had been almost at a standstill in Britain during the interregnum, but not in Europe, where the use of silver had been constantly spreading to include objects which had not existed before. Britain thus had a great deal of leeway to make up, but as there was insufficient bullion available to satisfy the demands of a booming industry, the insatiable national mania, which again affected inn-keepers, eventually contributed to a serious financial crisis. This is dealt with in the text under the heading 'Britannia standard'.

Matters improved in the early 18th century, partly owing to the issue of notes by the Bank of England, but it must not be forgotten that silverware in outmoded styles continued to be sacrificed to provide the necessary metal for plate of newer fashion, and many people had 17th-century silver utensils melted down 'On modern models to be wrought'.

An important technical improvement occurred in 1727. This was the invention of the flatting mill by John Cook, though it was not deve-loped to any extent until shortly before the middle of the century after the expiry of Cook's patent. Prior to this, silver had been reduced laboriously from the ingot to sheet by a team of men with sledge-hammers, but the flatting mill, or rolling mill as it would now be called, performed the task better and with less demand on skill and muscle. The sheet produced was more homogeneous in structure and had no hammer-marks which needed removal. Birmingham in parti-cular exploited this and other mechanical innovations with a foresight and vigour which resulted in a reduction in the cost of wrought plate and its consequent distribution more widely throughout British society. The experienced amateur of old plate will always prefer an object which has been raised in one piece to one which consists of rolled components soldered together, but there is no doubt that the production of the latter brought many attractive pieces of domestic silver within the reach of people who would otherwise have been unable to afford it.

Much old English, Scottish and Irish silver has found its way to the United States of America but, from time to time, a certain quantity returns across the Atlantic for sale in London auction-rooms. It will be some time before prices reach again the hysterical heights of 1968, but there is no doubt that old plate forms a sound investment as well as being delightful to possess and use for its own sake.

A short section on Medical silver has been included in this book, but more work remains to be done on the subject and for this, the co-operation of interested members of the medical profession will be necessary.

No attempt has been made to provide lists of either makers' marks or hall marks, as both are very adequately covered by certain existing publications mentioned in the Bibliography.

A

Aberdeen: plate was made in Aberdeen for four hundred years from the middle of the 15th century. Supervision of the craft was of a sporadic nature and hall-marking was never entirely standardised. Marks included at various times the initials AB, ABD and ABDN, but three small castles in a shield sometimes appeared and care should be taken

Aberdeen

not to confuse this mark with that of Newcastle upon Tyne. Very little plate of the more important kind seems to have been made in Aberdeen, but it has been included because spoons and forks are sometimes encountered. The metal used always approximated to the legal standard and workmanship was highly competent.

Acanthus: leaves of the plant *acanthus spinosus* were used in ancient Greek architecture in conventionalised form and are familiar on the capitals of Corinthian columns. The motif began to be used on English plate in the first half of the 16th century when the renaissance (q.v.) style was introduced and was never entirely neglected thereafter. It was probably applied most effectively in the reign of Charles II (1660–1685), when it often appeared, alternating with leaves of a plainer kind, round the bases of two-handled cups, beakers, tankards (q.q.v.) etc. During the classical revival in the late 18th century (*see* Adam) when leaf-forms were again widely used, the motif took on a noticeable stiffness and formality.

Adam, Robert (1728–1792): Scottish architect, born at Kirkcaldy in Fife and trained by his architect father, William Adam. He had three brothers, John, James and William, but Robert was the most outstanding member of a gifted family and was chiefly responsible for the introduction of the neo-classical or classical-revival style into Great Britain from 1758. In that year, he returned from a four-year visit to Italy, where he had encountered the sensation caused in archaeological circles – which included Sir William Hamilton – by the increasing discoveries made during the excavations of Herculaneum and Pompeii. Effective work on the first, which is not completed even yet, partly owing to the fact that the populous commune of Resina was built later over the ruins, had begun in 1738; at Pompeii, where much remains to be done also, excavations began in 1755. Both were classical cities near Naples, founded in about 500 B.C., which came under Roman domination just over four centuries later and thus embodied manifestations of all the succeeding styles from classical Greek to imperial Roman. Both were overwhelmed simultaneously by an eruption of Mt. Vesuvius in A.D. 79 and were buried under layers of volcanic mud, ash, or lava. Any life remaining in them was destroyed and pathetic evidences of this may be seen in the Naples museum, but the cities themselves were largely preserved by their unwelcome protective covering, which not only kept out the elements but also prevented local populations from using them as quarries for building material.

Hitherto, knowledge of classical ornament and artefacts had been derived chiefly from such original buildings as remained standing in various places and from traditions which were not wholly reliable, but now, for the first time, direct evidence was available. Here, as the débris slowly yielded to pick and shovel, were visible temples, homes, shops, taverns and even houses of ill-fame, all containing in varying degree furniture, utensils, ornaments and sometimes encaustic wall-paintings, often of a highly evidential character.

Adam returned to practise in London inspired with the same enthusiasm which affected the rest of western Europe, and a determination to adapt certain earlier, lighter phases of the classical idiom to contemporary usage. Like William Kent, one of the protagonists of the Palladian revival in the first half of the 18th century, he considered that an architect ought properly to design, not only a building, but all its more important contents as well in order to maintain stylistic consistency. He accordingly designed 'furniture' in the contemporary wide sense of the term, that is, anything with which a house is furnished, and this included not only chairs, sideboards, light-fittings, carpets, chimney-pieces and so forth, but also domestic plate.

It was not long before he began to receive commissions from wealthy clients and came to be regarded as an arbiter of taste; his designs exerted a vast influence, so that Sir John Soane was not exaggerating when he wrote later that Adam had brought about a revolution in art. The repertoire of neo-classical ornament was drawn upon in all the useful arts, so that the same decoration was employed notably in connection with architecture, furniture and plate. This ornament consisted chiefly of the following elements: swags or festoons (q.v.), rams' heads, bead mouldings (q.v.), paterae (q.v.), medallions (q.v.), stiff leafage, fluting, urns, satyrs' masks, the anthemion (q.v.) and husks, while a novel type of surface treatment on silver appeared in the form of bright-cut engraving (q.v.).

Apart from the various kinds of ornament, to which all exponents of the style maintained a general allegiance in their work, certain characteristic forms were used. For the silversmiths of the late 18th century, the most useful of original classical objects was undoubtedly the urn (q.v.), either with or without handles. (*See* Cups, two-handled.) The form of this vessel needed very little adaptation to render it suitable as a basis for the design of two-handled cups, hot-water jugs, goblets, coffee-pots, sauce tureens, soup tureens, sugar vases, bowls and baskets, tea-urns, tea-caddies, salt-cellars and argyles (q.q.v.). There were, of course, no classical counterparts for most of these productions of a more sophisticated age, and some of the items were not wholly satisfactory from a practical standpoint. Nevertheless, despite the long popularity of the preceding rococo style (q.v.), whose plastic qualities exerted a lasting appeal, it was fighting a rearguard action and suddenly fell completely out of favour in about 1770, under the relentless pressure of the style which Robert Adam had done so much to inaugurate. Neo-classical buildings were going up on an increasing scale and everything operated in favour of change, including the sale by Sir William Hamilton in 1772 of his collection of classical vases to the British Museum and the opening of the Etruria pottery by Josiah Wedgwood in 1769.

The Adam style remained virtually unchallenged until the end of the 18th century and even persisted to some extent after 1800, but signs of a reaction had already begun to appear. The powerful interrelationship between the arts ensured that any influence affecting one of them would inevitably affect the others sooner or later. In the last decade of the century, some work based in some degree on the French *Directoire* style, carried out by the architect Henry Holland at Carlton House, inspired Walpole to eulogistic comment and prompted him to refer to the Adam style in terms of scathing contempt. 'How sick one shall be', he wrote, 'after this chaste palace, of Mr Adam's gingerbread and sippets of embroidery.' The criticism was, of course, grossly unjust, and in contrasting, unconsciously, the feminine grace of the Adam style with the coarser masculinity of the nascent Regency taste, the commentator was doing little but expressing his own boredom with a well-disciplined system which had at last become wearisome to the novelty-seeking society in which he lived. Looking back over a longer perspective, however, we can see that the style which owed its introduction so much to the exertions of Robert Adam was one of the greatest in the history of the English arts including silversmithing, and although certain items of plate, including tea-pots (q.v.) had begun to abandon their loyalty to this style by the end of the 18th century, a consideration of what followed during the Regency and after leaves us with an unquiet feeling that progress is not necessarily commensurate with the passage of time.

Alms dish: a large dish on which church offerings were placed for consecration; usually of brass but occasionally of silver.

Andirons: silver-mounted andirons or fire-dogs were known in the royal household in the early 16th century, but most surviving examples were made between the restoration of the Monarchy in 1660, when their use became widespread, and about 1720. Throughout this period, although the horizontal bars to support the logs continued to be made of iron for obvious reasons, the uprights were usually of solid silver. Until the end of the 17th century treatment was often highly decorative, but thereafter, designs displayed greater sobriety, relying for their effect on satisfying forms and proportions rather than surface ornament. They were usually under noticeable Dutch influence.

Annealing: the softening of silver by heating it to a dull red heat, allowing it to lose its redness and then quenching it in water. Periodic annealing is necessary when shaping with the raising hammer, to prevent the metal becoming springy and cracking.

Anthemion

Anthemion: ornamental motif of classical origin consisting of formalised versions of the honeysuckle flower; introduced in the classical-revival period in the late 18th century and used chiefly as border decoration, bounded by bead mouldings. It continued to be used in the early 19th century.

Argyle, c. 1790

Argyle: a pot, with a handle and a spout like that of a tea-pot, for keeping gravy hot, deriving its name from the 4th Duke of Argyll who

17

is thought to have introduced it. Heat was provided either by a billet of hot iron in a cylindrical sleeve or by water either in an encircling jacket or a horizontal compartment. Argyles were prevalent in the late 18th and early 19th centuries. They may have declined in popular esteem owing to the difficulty of keeping them clean compared with normal sauce-boats or sauce-tureens (q.q.v.).

Asparagus-tongs: *see* Tongs, asparagus.

Assay: the testing of silver to ascertain its quality. In the period with which we are concerned two methods were employed, the first involving the use of a touchstone, the second, a cupel. A touchstone consisted of a piece of smooth 'Lydian stone' or basanite, which was a black siliceous jasper or schist. It was of fine grain but strongly abrasive, so that when a piece of silver to be tested was rubbed on it, some of the metal was transferred to the stone in a bright streak. This was compared with another streak of known quality. Cupellation was more scientific and less open to error. The cupel was a small bone-ash crucible and into this was placed a weighed scraping, taken from the object submitted for assay, wrapped in lead. When put in a furnace, the base metals present, comprising the easily fusible lead and the copper with which the silver was alloyed, were absorbed into the crucible leaving a droplet of pure silver. By comparing the weight of this with that of the original scraping, the quality could be accurately determined. If a piece of wrought plate was found to be below the legal standard, it was cut or battered and returned to the maker. *See* Hall-marking.

Assay cup: a small cup, known also as a cup of assay, used in great households by a trusted servant to sample his master's wine as a pre-caution against poisoning. These cups were used from the middle ages to the early 18th century, but evidence concerning them is purely documentary, so that we can have no definite idea of their appearance. Several are mentioned in the royal inventory of 1725, and as one was stated to be accompanied by a salver (q.v.) it is possible that the later versions were in the form of diminutive two-handled cups. Descriptions of wine-tasters are very similar and it seems likely that the two were often identical and differed only in the purpose to which they were put.

B

Barnstaple: silversmiths were operating in Barnstaple in Devon from before 1400 to the end of the 17th century. The first mark, used up to the end of the reign of James I (1603–1625), consisted of a bird in a circular stamp. This was followed by a triple-towered gatehouse which had a lowered portcullis up to the middle of the century. Thereafter, the word BARUM occurred in the stamp, the first three letters being above and the last two below. Sometimes, this mark also included the initials of a maker, but marking was often incomplete. It is improbable that much Barnstaple plate travelled far from Devon.

Baroque: a French term, probably deriving from the Spanish *barrueco*, a misshapen pearl, meaning originally something fanciful and freakish. In the second half of the 19th century it came to indicate the styles and ornament of the late renaissance (q.v.), which were superseded by the rococo style in the first half of the 18th century.

Basin: the most important examples of silver basins were accompanied by ewers (q.v.) and were used in noble and wealthy households for personal ablutions from the middle ages. It is recorded by a commentator of the early 16th century (George Cavendish) that, in Cardinal Wolsey's palace of Hampton Court 'Every chamber had a bason & an yewer of silver & some clean gylt and some parcell (*partly*) gylt.' At a time when it was not uncommon for nobles and prelates to possess vast accumulations of plate, there were no doubt many other great houses where Wolsey's displays could be matched but, for the most part, silver basins performed a practical and ceremonious function as containers for water in which the hands were washed before and after meals. Before forks (q.v.) became more widely distributed from about

19

1660, it had been the custom to eat with the fingers, which accordingly became coated with fat, gravy and so forth. At the end of a meal a basin and ewer were brought round by a servant so that diners could wash their hands and clean their teeth with a napkin dipped in the water. A 15th-century English work, designed to teach children good manners, recommended them not to spit in the basin after completing their ablutions. After the general adoption of forks, basins ceased to be used in the above manner in most households, but continued nevertheless to be made as presentation pieces, when their purpose was chiefly ostentatious. Virtually, the earliest surviving secular examples date from the 16th century, many of them being decorated in the prevailing renaissance style. A highly ornamented garniture, made by Paul Lamerie in the first half of the 18th century, is still part of the magnificent collection of plate belonging to the Worshipful Company of Goldsmiths, but it is doubtful if it was ever used for its ostensible purpose. Very few such basins were made after 1750. *See* also Basin, shaving.

Basin, shaving: it is clear from documentary sources that silver shaving-bowls, dishes or 'basons' were known in the second half of the 15th century and may well have existed before, but we know nothing of their appearance except that they were circular and some were of large size: the second fact being deducible from the weight. The earliest survivors date from the late 17th century, though all are exceedingly rare. They were either circular or oval, with a crescent-shaped gap for the neck in the flat brim which might be a third of the width of the central hollow. These basins were mostly devoid of all decoration apart from a simple moulding round the edge. *See* also Jugs, shaving.

Baskets, bread: *see* Baskets, table.

Baskets, cake: *see* Baskets, table.

Baskets, sugar: these first appeared in about 1770 and were an open variant of contemporary sugar-bowls, the word 'basket' being applied to them on account of the pierced decoration which often occurred and the fact that they frequently had arched swing-handles. It is probable that most of them were originally equipped with glass liners. Nearly all were mounted on stems and feet, whether the bodies were in the form of urns or of a low boat-shape. In the first years of the 19th century a few sugar baskets were of a rounded oblong form with outward-bulging sides like many contemporary tea-pots (q.v.), but thereafter, the incidence of pierced decoration of late 18th-century type declined very quickly. Some of this decoration consisted of fairly simple palings, occasionally with a slight Gothic flavour, but sometimes included typical neo-classical elements such as swags, medallions, paterae, etc. Borders and handles were usually beaded.

Baskets, sweetmeat: these were in the form of miniature table baskets (*see* Baskets, table) and were of similar appearance. They were sometimes suspended by the handles from the branches of centrepieces (q.v.) especially in the late 18th century, baskets of this kind being often provided with foot-rings instead of feet.

Table basket, c. 1740

Baskets, table: these are often described either as bread-baskets or cake-baskets, but as it is probable that the owner of such a piece of plate

21

would have put it to any reasonable purpose he chose, the name 'table basket', which occurred in a royal inventory of 1725, seems the most suitable.

They were already in use in the late 16th century, but surviving examples made before the early 18th century are extremely rare. Those in the Queen Anne period were either oval or circular, the sides, pierced with various designs such as scales or lattice, widening from base to rim. They were usually finished with heavily moulded edges and were provided with handles. An uncommon type which appeared about 1740 was shaped like a large shell, while others simulated actual basket-work, but the majority originating in the middle decades of the century were in the rococo style, which suited the character of table baskets very well. They were generally mounted on four feet and were equipped with swing-handles, arching across the width of the oval or rounded oblong bodies, and thereafter this kind of handle was practically universal.

Table baskets of the Adam period were disappointing compared with their predecessors in the rococo style. Most of them stood on foot-rings, soldered beneath the base, or on the base itself if it was flat. The piercing which decorated the sides was usually of a perfunctory, uninspired nature and the metal was often very thin. These frequently suggest mass-production methods, but some better examples were embellished with applied neo-classical ornament such as swags and small medallions, while bead-mouldings often occurred on the handles and borders of even the plainest. A slightly atypical version had a handle something after the fashion of a chain and sides consisting of vertical palings, widely spaced, with applied stalks and ears of wheat. These can be recognized as belonging to the same period less by their ornament than their flimsiness, though they were undoubtedly more craftsmanlike and pleasing than their contemporaries made of pierced sheet metal. A modified rendering of the latter, often without any piercing at all, persisted into the early 19th century, but it seems that after this the manufacture of table baskets declined. The best of all were undoubtedly those of the rococo period, while the most numerous date from the late 18th and early 19th centuries. Whatever the style of ornament, the bases of table baskets were always made of solid silver to prevent the shedding of crumbs.

Basting spoon: *see* Spoon, basting.

Beading, Bead moulding: a type of border decoration consisting of a row of contiguous small hemispheres looking somewhat like a string of beads, the introduction of which dates effectively from the advent of the neo-classical style in the late 18th century. It proved very popular, sometimes playing an ancillary role to other ornament, sometimes occurring by itself. It was found on plate of all kinds including flatware (q.v.).

Beaker, c. 1580

Beaker: one of the most ancient of drinking vessels. It is generally supposed that the earliest were made from a cylindrical section of horn with a disc of the same material fixed into the smaller end to form a base. Beakers are frequently shown in English manuscript illustrations of the 11th century, and although their substance cannot be deduced from such sources, the Anglo-Saxon goldsmiths already enjoyed something of an international reputation, so that there can be little doubt that they must have made beakers of silver as well as standing cups and other objects. During its long history, the basic form of the beaker underwent little change though there was some variation in proportion, while ornament, if any, naturally accorded with the prevailing style. It always consisted essentially of a cylindrical body, widening from base to rim, with either straight or concave sides and with a flat disc of silver forming the base of the receptacle. It was almost invariably supported on a moulded foot-ring which raised the bottom of the vessel above table-level, and might also have a narrow, moulded girdle soldered round the body, usually about the middle. From the time of its first appearance until the late 16th century, some examples might be equipped with covers in common with many other vessels. In the middle ages, these covers were either conical or hemispherical, sometimes with battlemented rims in the Gothic period, but the former shape went out of favour with the introduction of the renaissance style, and thereafter covers were of domed formation.

It is known from documentary and pictorial sources that silver beakers were popular and widely distributed in the 16th century, but there are few survivors dating from before 1550. Those of the Elizabethan period (1558–1603) were of two main kinds, one of which was frequently decorated by embossing, the other with engraving. The first, which had appeared in the first half of the century and is extremely rare, had straight sides widening towards the rim, the base of the body being slightly recessed above the foot. The domed cover and body were usually embossed in high relief with the Germanic fruit motifs common at the period on other silver objects, the whole being normally finished by gilding, by the ancient mercury process. This type of beaker is often called a 'Magdalen cup' because it is of similar appearance to the vessel containing the ointment in many late medieval and renaissance paintings of Mary Madgalen. In addition to individual beakers, others were made in nests of up to ten or possibly more. Each beaker was encircled near the top by a narrow applied moulding which rested on the rim of the one below. The topmost vessel usually had a hemispherical cover and sometimes looked like a Magdalen cup.

More common than any of these, were individual beakers with smoothly flaring, concave sides, devoid of embossing but bearing engraved ornament in the upper half. This ornament nearly always included a horizontal zone below the rim, bounded by strapwork bands which often crossed over at intervals, containing floral and foliate scrolls sometimes with occasional heads. Below this narrow, upper zone, the scrollwork thinned out into points in the direction of the base and sometimes embodied shields of arms or vases of flowers. The foot-ring was widely expansive and stamped by means of repeating dies with small-scale renaissance ornament such as egg-and-dart, gadroons, or acanthus leaves. These beakers were seldom gilded, possibly because their smoothness of surface made it easy to keep the metal free from tarnish (silver sulphide), but possibly also because their use extended well down through the social scale and the absence of gilding reduced the cost. They were offered, with noticeable frequency, as prizes in the Elizabethan state lottery, which was designed to raise funds for the upkeep of maritime harbours.

Magdalen cup, c. 1560

They persisted into the early 17th century, when some of them found their way into churches for use as communion cups, a purpose for which their narrowness and height made them quite unsuitable. In the reign of James I (1603-1625), they tended to become shorter and the foot-ring was replaced by narrow mouldings, sloping outward only very slightly, while the engraved ornament, while drawing on the same sources as previously, became careless and degenerate. Some were quite plain in accordance with the prevailing tendency to leave plate unadorned, and gilding became almost unknown, but the narrowness of the moulded foot-rings indicates a post-Elizabethan date despite the absence of evidence otherwise furnished by the engraved ornament.

The same stylistic tendencies continued through the reign of Charles I (1625–1649) and possibly the Commonwealth, though the joyless era when those in the ascendancy based their attitudes on the Old Testament rather than the Christian Bible has afforded too few examples for any firm deductions to be made. The restoration of the Monarchy in 1660 brought about certain changes, due primarily to Dutch influence. Proportions were unaffected, but decoration, when it occurred, consisted characteristically of embossed botanical ornament of a bold and florid nature, which often included large tulip leaves and blossoms. Of lower incidence but greatly superior, was an alternative type of decoration which was found more frequently on other kinds of hollowware such as tankards and two-handled cups (q.q.v.). This comprised a circuit of acanthus and other leaves, rising from the base just above the foot-ring and terminating at a varying distance below the middle.

The leaf-and-flower ornament on beakers remained prevalent throughout the reigns of Charles II (1660–1685) and James II (1685–1689), but under William and Mary was superseded by elements popularised by immigrant Huguenot silversmiths who had fled from France to escape the persecutions which followed the revocation of the Edict of Nantes by Louis XIV in 1685. Alternate gadroons and flutes (q.q.v.), usually slightly spiralled, extended vertically from the base to about halfway up the body and, above this, a short distance below the rim, was a cabled horizontal moulding deeply embossed from the inside. Each side of this moulding and just above the gadroons, the transition from decorated to plain surfaces was eased by small stamped motifs such as strawberry leaves. The same kind of ornament occurred on other contemporary objects as well and remained popular throughout the reign of Queen Anne, who succeeded William III in 1702, and persisted in less degree through that of her successor, George I (1714–1727). Thereafter, although examples were found during the remainder of the 18th century, the incidence of beakers seems to have declined, and the comparatively few that were made were plain. Many were very small and were presumably intended for use by children. There was nothing in their appearance which provides any evidence of period and it is accordingly necessary to rely on the hall marks in this connection. *See* also Tumblers and Vases.

Bell: with minor exceptions, the only silver bells for secular use were made to accompany toilet sets or standishes (q.q.v.). Virtually none has survived from before the reign of Charles II. These bells were small, of normal shape and with a handle, usually baluster-shaped, of silver, wood or ivory, extending vertically from the top. Their purpose was to summon servants.

Bellows: silver or silver-mounted bellows may possibly have existed prior to 1660, but if so, none has survived. After the Restoration, when the use of plate was extending over an ever-widening field, andirons (q.v.) and other fireplace requisites were sometimes made of silver. The Duke of Lauderdale owned a silver bellows at Ham House and another is at Windsor Castle, but these objects are now of the utmost rarity.

Berry spoon: a jargon name applied to a table spoon or dessert spoon embossed from beneath the bowl with fruit ornament and with the interior usually gilded. Plain Georgian silver spoons first began to be slighted in this manner in the Victorian period, but no such spoons existed at the dates indicated by the hall marks. It is believed that the practice still continues, to satisfy a demand by uninformed persons who are not aware that such spoons have been spoilt and are not in their original state. Amateurs of old silver are strongly recommended to leave such objects alone.

Biggin: a cylindrical coffee-pot or percolator of the early 19th century, possibly named after its inventor.

Birmingham: it is not known when silversmithing activities in Birmingham and its vicinity first attained any considerable volume, but there is no doubt that this stage had been reached by 1773. In February of that year a petition was presented to Parliament on behalf of the Birmingham plate-workers, asking permission to establish an assay office and referring to the similar petition presented the day before by Sheffield (q.v.). The procedure was obviously both collusive and tactically sound. Hitherto, it had been necessary for all wrought plate to be sent for assay to Chester or London, and attention was drawn to the resultant delay, inconvenience and expense. The Goldsmiths' Company of London, jealous of their privileges and anxious to suffer no diminution of their revenues from assaying, put up a strong resistance to the petition, but the parliamentary commission which heard their objections evidently concluded that their attitude was not inspired entirely by altruism, and the petition went forward. An Act was then passed appointing Birmingham as an assay town and establishing a Company called 'The Guardians of the Standard of Wrought Plate in Birmingham', with statutory jurisdiction over all silversmithing in the town itself and within thirty miles.

A prime mover in the campaign was the distinguished manufacturer Matthew Boulton, a man of scientific as well as artistic interests, friend of Joseph Priestley and a member of the somewhat alchemical Lunar Society satirised by William Blake. He was a great organiser and was responsible for the introduction of mass-production methods which, without lowering quality, reduced the cost of plate so that it became available to a wider public. His own and other firms also supplied ready-made parts (findings) for assembly by silversmiths elsewhere, so that it is quite possible that many tea-pots, for example, stamped with London marks, underwent the basic stages of manufacture in Birmingham and were later completed by London firms who sponsored them at Goldsmiths' Hall.

The mark chosen by Birmingham was an anchor, and it seems likely that, as the representatives of Birmingham and Sheffield carried out their deliberations at the famous Crown and Anchor tavern in the Strand, they divided the elements of the tavern-sign between them, Birmingham taking the anchor and Sheffield the crown.

Blackjack: a drinking pot with a single handle, made of jacked or stiffened leather. From the late 17th century they were sometimes provided with rims and feet of silver and a silver escutcheon on the side opposite the handle. Occasional examples were completely lined with silver also: an enhancement which, since it involved the use of no less precious metal than that contained in a mug or can, probably bears witness to an improvement in the owner's fortunes as well as to the affection with which he regarded his blackjack.

Bleeding bowl or Cupping bowl: in the 17th and 18th centuries, when the therapeutic value of cupping or bleeding enjoyed a somewhat inflated reputation, shallow pewter or silver bowls with single lugs or handles, were often used for the purpose in hospitals and by private surgeons. These bowls were not specially made for surgical use, but were ordinary contemporary porringers, engraved inside with graduation lines to measure the number of ounces of blood taken from a patient. The name should therefore be applied only if the engraved lines are present. *See* Porringer and Medical silver.

Blowhole: a hole in cast work or solder caused by the escape of hot air. Blowholes are sometimes to be seen round the base of the body of a mug, tankard etc., in the solder used to attach the inside of the foot-ring.

Bottle-stand: a silver stand for a bottle or decanter, usually in the form of a shallow bowl. Bottle-stands probably first appeared in the second quarter of the 18th century. They were the ancestors of the more numerous coasters (q.v.) of the Adam period and later.

Bottle ticket, c. 1740

Bottle ticket: the original and correct term for the silver labels, suspended round the necks of decanters by thin chains, engraved or pierced with the name of the contents. There is a modern tendency to call them 'wine labels', but as they often bear such names as whisky, gin, rum, brandy, shrub, or strong ale, none of which is a wine, the usage is manifestly inaccurate and undesirable. Bottle tickets were first made in the second quarter of the 18th century, the earliest being in the form of wide escutcheons. They were seldom fully marked until after 1790, early examples usually having only the maker's mark and the quality mark, generally Sterling. Even these, however, can be dated approximately according to the normal working life of the maker and the shape of the cartouche enclosing the lion passant. The first can be ascertained in most cases by reference to Sir Charles Jackson's *English Goldsmiths and their Marks* and the second will be found in any reliable list of hall marks such as Bradbury's *British and Irish Silver Assay Office Marks*. *See* Hall-marking.

Bowl: the receptacle of a standing cup, two-handled cup etc., as distinct from other parts such as stems, feet, or handles. *See* Bowl, drinking; Bowl, punch etc.

Drinking bowl, c. 800

Bowl, drinking: a short drinking vessel, standing on its own base or on a stem and foot of the most rudimentary kind. Drinking bowls were evidently popular in Anglo-Saxon England and several, both with and without covers, have survived from the pre-Conquest era beginning with the 9th century. The fact that the nationality of nearly all of them is uncertain is of no great importance, as it merely indicates that Anglo-Saxon styles showed a close affinity with those of Germanic northern

30

Europe in general. These early bowls were of two main kinds: one was shaped rather like a bird's nest, with sides expanding in a convex curve so that the top was considerably wider than the base, the other curved slightly inward from base to rim so that it was narrower at the top. The second type may have been inspired by Oriental originals, for the shape was common among Islamic coppersmiths and may have reached northern Europe through the Swedish Vikings, to whom the eastern Mediterranean and the Black Sea were well known. Some connection, however tenuous, undoubtedly existed between Britain and the East for, in the middle of the 19th century, a Celtic treasure-hoard discovered in Orkney was found to include 10th-century coins from Baghdad. Some Anglo-Saxon ornament, particularly interlacing strapwork (q.v.), also had a certain Islamic flavour.

Various decorative techniques were employed, including gilding, embossing, chasing, engraving, carving and the use of niello (q.q.v.). Designs, in addition to strapwork, consisted chiefly of twining branches or scrolls which sometimes terminated in monsters' heads, fishes, animals, birds and grotesque masks.

Little is known about the incidence of drinking bowls throughout the rest of the middle ages. The paucity of survivors could be due to various causes, including the destruction attendant upon changes in style, theft, or sequestration during the Civil War, or they may simply have gone out of general fashion. However, a 14th-century example of bird's-nest shape, the Studley Bowl, is preserved in the Victoria & Albert Museum in London, and is an object of great distinction. It still retains its cover, which is in the form of a compressed cone, and is mounted on a wide silver cylinder, too short to be called a stem. It is engraved with foliage and the letters of an incomplete medieval alphabet, and the original gilding is still largely intact.

In the 15th century, a low goblet with a trumpet-shaped stem was sometimes found, but as the stem was short rather then rudimentary, the type is considered under Cups, standing.

From the earliest times there had been a tendency to mount non-metallic substances in silver or silver-gilt, a familiar example being the drinking horn. In the early 16th century, one such substance was Cornish serpentine marble, a veined stone of dark green colour which made a dramatic tonal contrast with gold and silver. Bowls of serpentine, having much the same appearance as mazers (q.v.), were provided with deep lip-bands and low feet of silver or silver-gilt which were crimped over projecting surfaces on the marble. It is possible that bowls

31

of this sort owe their survival partly to the fact that the comparatively small quantity of precious metal used in their manufacture made it unprofitable to steal them or detach the silver for melting. At all events, drinking bowls entirely of silver dating from this time onwards are virtually unknown, though documentary references indicate that a great many must have been in circulation. William Harrison, writing in 1587 and describing the improvement in economic conditions in the agricultural community, spoke of a typical tenant farmer as having 'a silver salt, a bowl for wine (if not a whole nest), and a dozen of spoons to furnish up the suit'. It is possible, however, that their use was practically confined to the less wealthy classes, for there is no doubt that other contemporary drinking vessels were more convenient to use. The possibility must also be faced that some of them may have had stems and feet added to them later to convert them into standing cups. *See* also Mazer.

Punch-bowl, c. 1720

Bowl, punch: ceramic bowls were used for the brewing of punch soon after it was introduced into England in about 1630 by Englishmen returning from the East, but the bowls do not appear to have been made of silver before 1660. The name of the drink derives ultimately from a Sanskrit word *pañca*, meaning five, with reference to the number of essential ingredients: water, sugar, limes or lemons, spices and spirit, the last generally consisting of brandy for some years. A 17th-century round by Henry Purcell begins: 'Bring the bowl and cool Nantz and let us be mixing', 'Nantz' being a contemporary colloquialism for brandy, probably because it was exported through the port of Nantes on the Loire. Rum, or a mixutre of rum and brandy, became popular later.

Early silver punch-bowls had no moulding round the upper edge, but after the introduction of the monteith (q.v.) in 1683, one bowl was sometimes made to serve both purposes, and this tendency gained ground with the passage of time until about 1720. Finish became more sophisticated, largely owing to the influence of immigrant Huguenot silversmiths who worked in a lavish and expensive manner to attract a wealthy clientele and made many monteiths, which were objects of luxury. They conferred a monumental aspect upon them by the use of such elements as cast and applied mouldings, classical masks, gadrooning, especially on the feet, and ring-handles pivoted from the jaws of lions' masks, one on each side. These handles were common on monteiths but were often lacking on bowls dedicated only to punch. In order to compete with the resourceful immigrants, native craftsmen were obliged to adopt a similar mode of working, but it must be admitted that their detail was sometimes coarser and less carefully finished.

By 1690, very few people considered it desirable to possess both a monteith and a separate bowl for punch as well, and a modified vessel was devised which was suitable for either purpose. An inconvenience which must have attached to the use of an ordinary monteith for punch was that it could be easily overfilled, so that liquor ran over the edge through the irrelevant indentations, but the new type was provided with a detachable rim having something of the appearance of a crown. When this was in position, the bowl was manifestly doing duty as a monteith, but when it was removed, the level rim of the vessel made it suitable for punch. At the same time, another form of surface treatment became popular, the outsides of many bowls being covered with vertical fluting. This decoration remained prevalent through the first two decades of the 18th century, some of the bowls to which it was applied having a tap near the base; but in about 1720, the silver monteith fell out of favour altogether and the punch-bowl continued thereafter in its own proper likeness. Decoration became rare, so that effect depended on good proportions and the uninterrupted sheen of the silver. Even in the rococo (q.v.) period, ornament usually consisted of nothing but a shaped cartouche containing the arms of the owner. Some modification in form occurred, with the rudimentary stem, which already existed between the base of the receptacle and the foot, increasing somewhat in height; but the incidence of silver punch-bowls seems to have declined in the second half of the 18th century, with the Adam period yielding surprisingly few examples. Some have survived from the Regency with fine reeding or gadrooning on the lower part of the body, and sometimes equipped with a cover with a hole on one side to accommodate the ladle, but these are seldom encountered. Pictorial and literary sources, however, indicate no diminution in the popularity of punch itself, but it seems likely that most people were content to serve it from bowls made of china or, less frequently, of glass.

Irish sugar-bowl, c. 1760

Bowl, sugar: the earliest surviving sugar-bowls date from the last decade of the 17th century, for although silver containers for sugar almost certainly existed before, bowls were usually connected with the service of tea, which did not become at all popular until after 1680. The first examples of which we have any knowledge were about 13 cm high, with sides curving in to the base which was mounted on a narrow foot-ring. They were of either circular or polygonal section and were equipped with domed or roughly pyramidal covers surmounted by small, solid finials often of ball-shape. These types persisted to some extent into the early 18th century, but were eventually superseded by shorter bowls, wider in relation to their height, with a concave moulding above the foot suggestive of an incipient stem. Most of the covers, either plain or decorated *en suite* with the bowls, were topped by moulded rings which formed feet when the covers were inverted so that they could be used as spoon-trays or saucers. They are sometimes considered as having been intended as stands for tea-pots, but this seems unlikely in view of their comparative instability, which would render them undesirable in association with boiling-hot liquid. Much

34

the same type continued through the middle decades of the 18th century, sometimes embossed with rococo (q.v.) ornament, but some of the most satisfying sugar-bowls of this period were Scottish or Irish. These were usually without covers and with hemispherical bodies with everted rims, the former being mounted on a low foot and the latter on three short legs often of cabriole shape and with a lion's mask at the point of attachment. Some of the Irish ones were decorated with low-relief rococo or other ornament, while plainer specimens had widely-spaced narrow flutes on the outside.

In the Adam period, both main forms of the ubiquitous classical urn were pressed into service, some being like large egg-cups with swing-handles, mounted on stems and feet, others looking something like boats, with lower, wider bodies curving up at the ends. All were liable to have pierced sides (*see* Basket, sugar). Homogeneous tea-sets had become widely popular by this time, and at the end of the 18th century sugar-bowls were commonly of the same shape as the other objects in the set. Most of them were provided with vertical loop-handles with rounded tops, but square tops became more usual in the early 19th century. At the same time, many were of rounded oblong shape with bulging sides, like a popular form of contemporary tea-pot, supported underneath on four ball-feet, while many, especially circular examples, had vertical gadroons on the lower part of the outside.

Box, snuff: the habit of taking snuff was copied originally from certain South-American tribes and was popular in 16th-century France where it seems to have been considered beneficial to the health. It became increasingly common in England during the 17th century, and a catch of the Charles-II period begins: 'Some write in the praise of tobacco and wine, while others praise women, but snuff shall be mine.' As snuff-taking became a national habit, silver was naturally among the materials used for containers, but it is often difficult to distinguish between boxes for snuff and those intended for tobacco. Nearly all, of the late 17th and early 18th centuries, were oval in form and often bore engraving of high quality. It is generally accepted that tobacco-boxes were often larger than snuff-boxes, but the line of demarcation between early 18th-century specimens is often difficult to recognize. Occasionally, snuff-boxes were divided into two compartments, presumably for different kinds of snuff, and a few freakish examples were equipped with small swing-out magnifying glasses for reading. In the early 19th century, some had small musical boxes in the base, but these were probably intended to be left on a table rather than carried on the person. In the rococo period, shapes varied considerably and provide an extensive field for the collector. Some of the snuff-boxes of this period were, in fact, considerable works of art, the decoration ranging from the formal to the pictorial, the latter sometimes consisting of battle scenes, usually depicting cavalry combats, embossed on separate plates which were soldered on to the lids. Most of these and other snuff-boxes were gilded internally. Those of the late 18th and early 19th centuries were generally of rectangular shape, often with simple, engine-turned ornament.

Soap-box, c. 1720

Box, soap: silver soap-boxes accompanying shaving or washing equipment in the late 17th and 18th centuries were either spherical or ovoid, mounted on round feet and with lids which were either plain, or pierced and engraved. A counterpart, in wood, often occurred on the mahogany basin stands of the mid-18th century, but surviving silver examples are surprisingly rare.

Box, spice: the name 'spice-box' is usually applied to certain silver caskets, shaped like scallop shells, of the late 16th and early 17th centuries, when the interior is divided into compartments by partitions. These attractive caskets were mounted on small feet, the convex lids

Spice-box, c. 1600

being embossed with the radiating ribs found on the outside of the shells from which they derived their inspiration. *See* Box, sugar.

Sugar-box, c. 1670

Box, sugar: two kinds of small silver caskets are usually described as sugar-boxes. (*a*) A box in the form of a scallop shell, identical in outward appearance to a spice-box (q.v.) but without internal compartments. (*b*) An oval, bun-shaped casket with a hinged lid secured by a hasp, mounted on four scrolled feet and originating about the middle of the 17th century. Both sugar-boxes and spice-boxes were later superseded by casters (q.v.).

Brandy saucepan: *see* Saucepan.

Bread-basket: *see* Basket, table.

Bright-cut engraving: the introduction of this type of engraving coincided with that of the Adam style (q.v.). It differed from ordinary linear engraving in that shallow flakes or chips were removed from the metal by means of a broader-ended graver, so that the cut surfaces reflected the light. It was applied to plate of all kinds including spoons and forks in the late 18th century.

Bristol: by an Act of 1423, Bristol was authorised to assay and mark plate and the authorisation was reiterated in 1700, but very little has survived which can be associated with the city. The hall mark was the city arms: a ship appearing from behind a castle, and there seems no doubt that date-letters were sometimes used; but too little is known of them for a reliable chronology to be established. Most surviving Bristol plate is to be found in the south-western part of England.

(a) Britannia mark. (b) Lion's head erased

Britannia metal: this base-metal alloy is mentioned only in case it should be confused with silver of the so-called Britannia standard (q.v.). It comprised tin, copper and antimony and was often used as a base for electro-plating in the 19th century.

Britannia standard: the usual name for the higher standard of silver which was compulsory for wrought plate between 27 March 1697 and 1 June 1720, and was indicated by a figure of Britannia. The Act of 1696 imposing the change was designed to increase the price of plate to discourage its purchase, and to make it impossible for silversmiths to use the coinage, which was of Sterling quality, as a raw material for their productions. The Britannia standard implied the presence, in 12 ounces (Troy) of metal, of $11\frac{1}{2}$ ounces of pure silver, as opposed to the $11\frac{1}{10}$ ounces of the Sterling standard. The Britannia mark was introduced to obviate confusion and, at the same time, a lion's head erased replaced the frontal lion's head as the London mark. Silversmiths were also obliged to enter new personal symbols consisting of the first two letters of the surname. At the time of the Act, England found herself in the grip of a serious financial crisis. A number of factors had contributed to this, but one was undoubtedly the national mania for collecting plate, which prompted many people to take bags of coins to silversmiths for melting. The circumstances also encouraged the capital offence of coin-clipping, and John Evelyn, the diarist, had written concerning this in 1694: 'many executed at London for clipping money, now done to that intolerable extent, that there was hardly any money that was worth above half the nominal value'. The Act did not apply either to Scotland or Ireland, where Sterling silver continued to be used, but great distress was caused in the English provincial assay towns by the inadvertent omission of their names from the statute, so that they were deprived of the right to assay and mark plate of the new quality. This omission, which brought provincial assay-office activity to a standstill, was made good by Acts of 1700–1701. The statute of 1719 which repealed that of 1696 referred, in its preamble, to the fact that plate of the purer quality did not wear as well as Sterling, which was harder by reason of the slightly higher copper content. Because of this and for reasons of expense, a general return was made to Sterling in 1720, but it is necessary to remember that the Britannia standard ceased only to be compulsory and became optional, so that it continued to be used on occasion and is sometimes even found in modern times. This warning is very necessary, since a number of people are inclined to regard any piece of plate bearing the Britannia marks as having originated in the late 17th or early 18th centuries.

Buckle: many buckles were made of silver in former times, including those on sword-hangers of the 16th century, but shoe-buckles are the most important surviving class. Most of these were made in the late 18th century in Birmingham, which appears to have had a large trade in these items.

Butter-dish: silver butter-dishes may have existed before 1700, but if any have survived, they cannot be identified by their appearance. The only important examples are those which were made from the second quarter of the 18th century in the form of scallop shells, sometimes supported on three ball-feet. Some Irish specimens of the same period owed nothing to this source, but were pierced and lined with glass, the ornament often consisting, apart from formal mouldings, of rustic scenes such as cows being milked among foliage. The cover, decorated in a similar idiom, was sometimes surmounted by a finial in the form of a recumbent cow. Butter-dishes of the early 19th century were often straight-sided and of oval section, with a cover finished with a central knob and with a shallow stand on four small feet with a handle at each end.

C

Caddy: a term deriving from the Malay word *kati*, meaning a weight slightly less than 1¼ lb. Tea was sold in boxes containing this amount and, in the late 18th century, the term became transferred from the quantity to the container. Prior to this, from the time of their inception, silver tea-receptacles had been called canisters, but it is convenient to use the word caddy retrospectively. The earliest surviving examples date from the beginning of the 18th century. For many years, although they were sometimes made individually, they more commonly appeared in sets of two or three, sometimes accompanied by a sugar-bowl, and were shaped to fit into a case provided with a lock, the key being kept by the mistress of the house as a precaution against the pilfering of the expensive contents by servants. Early caddies were of simple form and pleasing design, one of the most popular being of an octagonal section which might be described as oblong with the corners clipped off. Others were oval, rectangular, or in the form of polygonal inverted balusters. Nearly all were flat-topped with a central hole having a domed cover and the majority had a sliding top or bottom for ease of filling. Just before the rococo period, some curvature began to occur more frequently in the profile which bulged outward in the upper half and, shortly after, many were embossed with rococo and chinoiserie (q.q.v.) ornament and some assumed the appearance of vases. These also, like the earlier varieties, might be made in sets of three, two being small and one large. The large one was sometimes

Caddy, c. 1715

provided with a small ladle which could be hung from one of the two handles. The bowl of the ladle was often fluted and pierced: a form of treatment which has occasionally caused them to be described as sugar-sifters, which would be of little use in connection with tea-drinking. In fact, this type of tea-ladle was the ancestor of the little caddy-spoons (q.v.) which began to appear in the last quarter of the 18th century.

In about 1760 another type of caddy was introduced, its currency overlapping that of the existing varieties. It was tall and cylindrical with a hinged cover, and held a large quantity of tea but, more popular than this, was a long caddy of oval or octagonal section, divided internally by partitions into three compartments. Despite the fact that tea had become progressively cheaper, it was still considered desirable for these caddies to have locks, and this feature continued to be found on many smaller examples of the late 18th century. The latter were of two main kinds. One was shaped like a classical urn, mounted on a stem and foot, and had an especially pleasing aspect. The other, which normally had a keyhole in one side, was of oval or polygonal section with vertical sides and looked somewhat like a contemporary tea-pot without spout or handle. The relationship with tea-pots persisted into the 19th century, with the more bulbous shapes characteristic of the Regency (q.v.), some being not unattractive, but late in this period there arose a taste for plethoric, confused ornament in high relief which clearly formed the advance-guard of the approaching decadence.

Caddy-spoon: *see* Spoon, caddy.

Can or Mug: a drinking vessel with a single handle like a tankard (q.v.), but without a lid. Literary references to cans occurred in the 16th century, for example, in a bibulous song which began; 'Now God be with old Simeon, for he made cans for many a one', but these were almost certainly of pewter. It seems probable, however, that silver cans were known in the first half of the 17th century, for a record of 1635 mentions, not only tankards, but also 'beere cups', which were presumably lidless vessels of the mug variety.

The earliest surviving English silver cans were made in the reign of Charles II, their form clearly deriving from that of a pottery vessel. They had globular bodies with short cylindrical necks which were usually chased with encircling parallel lines, probably to impart rigidity. The S-shaped handles, which consisted of ribbons of sheet silver, were of mean appearance and uncomfortable to hold on account of their thinness. These cans or mugs were nothing like contemporary tankards but, in the 1680s, they began to be made in the cylindrical form of their lidded relatives, with a capacity of about a pint. The globular variety continued for a short time after 1700, but the cylindrical type was more popular and of superior appearance. Its handle was hollow and of D-section, with a thumb-rest at the top where it joined the body. The latter was sometimes encircled, just below the rim, by a broad applied moulding in the late 17th century, but this moulding became narrower after 1700, its use being practically confined to the reign of Queen Anne (1702–1714). Thereafter, it was sometimes

Can, c. 1680

Can, c. 1690

Can, c. 1720

Can, c. 1750

Can, c. 1790

suggested by parallel, chased lines with a slightly embossed zone between them, but this feature did not last for long, and plain, cylindrical mugs continued throughout the 18th century despite the introduction of various other types. A baluster-shape also appeared before 1700 and continued to be made infrequently in the reign of Queen Anne. It began to become popular in the second quarter of the 18th century, but was probably not numerically superior to the cylindrical variety until after 1750, when the handle was usually cast and of single or double scroll form. A shape introduced in the reign of George I (1714–1727) scarcely persisted after 1730. The body was a hybrid between a cylinder and a baluster, the sides being almost straight but curving suddenly inward at the base just above the foot-ring. This kind of base is known in commercial circles as 'tucked in'. These mugs bear marks appropriate to both the Britannia and Sterling standards (q.q.v.), but mostly the latter, since the majority were made after 1720.

In the last quarter of the 18th century, a very rare type which had been first introduced in the middle of the century suddenly became popular. It was linked stylistically with certain contemporary tankards from the same source. The body was either cylindrical or shaped like a cask, sometimes with engraved vertical lines suggestive of barrel-staves, sometimes only with two horizontal bands or sets of engraved lines indicating hoops. The handles were generally hollow and of square section, the topmost portion being horizontal and the lower part either curving away from the base of the body below the point of attachment or merging in its outline. These mugs continued to be made after 1800, and were far more numerous than another variety whose self-conscious aestheticism made it seem somewhat unsuitable for beer. This new mug had a body shaped like a bucket, and a reeded loop-handle. It was usually cast by the *cire-perdue* process (q.v.) and ornamented with finely-executed fruiting vines and figures of naked children. Cans of this kind, which were conceived in accordance with the contemporary doctrinaire approach to late classical styles, were meritorious objects of art, but seldom large enough to contain a reasonable measure of anything but wine.

Candelabrum: an alternative name for a candlestick with branches. Candelabra were known in the medieval period and during the 16th century, but virtually none has survived apart from a late 16th-century specimen which, over the years, has turned up in the saleroom so often that it is clearly incapable of satisfying its purchasers for long. This is in the form of a cross made of rock crystal and silver-gilt and was probably unusual for its period, Survivals are fairly numerous from the early 18th century, the basic designs being thereafter identical with those of contemporary candlesticks (q.v.). It is evident that the latter were often converted into candelabra by the later addition of branches.

Candle-extinguisher: this existed in two forms, the earlier of which was also known as a douter. This was somewhat like a pair of scissors, with flat plates at the ends for squeezing the lighted wick. Examples in silver date from the late 17th century and are extremely rare, probably owing to the greater convenience of the alternative extinguisher. This was of conical shape and 18th-century survivals are fairly common. These extinguishers were mostly provided with a short vertical prong on one side which fitted into a socket attached to the shaft or handle of a chamber-candlestick (q.v.).

Candlestand: a stand, initially of tripod form, to support a candlestick or candelabrum. These objects were mostly of wood, but a few were made of silver in the second half of the 17th century.

Candlestick: it is clear from documentary evidence that domestic silver candlesticks were not uncommon from the 14th century onwards in England, but there are virtually no survivors dating from before the 17th century and very few which were made before 1660. No doubt the wholesale melting of plate which took place during the Civil War is largely responsible for this state of affairs. However, a type more often represented in brass in the mid-17th century was also made in silver, though examples are very sparse. This had a trumpet-shaped foot, rising up in the form of a narrow cylinder and provided with a central, circular drip-pan. Those of the Charles-II period were mostly in the form of classical columns or clustered columns of medieval type, standing on a square platform which was probably a relic of the earlier drip-pan. Below this, the stem spread out into the foot. The platform and the foot were usually square, as was the socket which surmounted the column and contained in the capital. The columnar shafts were of thin silver, filled with a resinous compound to resist denting. This type

Candlestick, c. 1670

Candlestick, c. 1700

Candlestick, c. 1760

Candlestick, c. 1775

persisted into the last decade of the century, but others in similar style showed various modifications in treatment. The small platform often had a rounded edge covered with narrow gadroons (q.v.) and the foot was decorated in the same manner, while the portion of the shaft immediately above this was frequently fluted. Capital, platform and foot might be circular or polygonal. A few such candlesticks were made in the early 18th century, but meanwhile, a greatly superior design, varying in detail, had been introduced from France. This type was of heavy, cast silver with a stem comprising bold, simple mouldings which commonly included some form of baluster. If they were of circular section, there was normally a shallow, saucer-like depression in the centre of the foot. Some were polygonal, with the angles running up from a low, pyramidal foot, over the mouldings to the socket.

Variations on these basic forms went on being manufactured into the reign of George II (1727–1760), generally becoming taller and more elaborate and, late in the period, spindly. The candlesticks of the rococo period were disappointing. The Queen-Anne style was by then a spent force and some hesitancy prevailed in design, with actual rococo ornament playing a surprisingly small part. Classical columns returned to favour, usually with Corinthian capitals, and detachable nozzles became common. Some of the columns were spirally wreathed with flowers or foliage. Apart from the last, all the columnar varieties lasted throughout the remainder of the 18th century into the Regency period and beyond, very often with bases loaded with lead and a baize-covered copper plate fixed into the foot. But meanwhile, from the time when the Adam style gained general recognition in about 1770, improvements had begun to manifest themselves and design took on a more assured, self-confident character. The shafts of many candlesticks were made in the form of classical pedestals of square, oval, or circular section, rising from feet of the same shape or occasionally triangular, and surmounted by sockets in the guise of urns. Some of the finest candlesticks of this era were made at Sheffield, which at times even supplied them to London silversmiths who sometimes had them re-assayed at Goldsmiths' Hall and overstruck with London marks. The latter process was sometimes executed rather carelessly, so that the original marks can still be deciphered.

Derivatives of pre-existing designs appeared in the 19th century, usually with more elaborate decoration than previously and with a good deal of cast and applied detail in accordance with the prevailing taste for massiveness. Strictly speaking, there was no true Regency type of candlestick, as designers were running out of ideas and often felt obliged to resuscitate outmoded styles including the rococo.

Canister: *see* Caddy.

Cassolet or Perfume-burner: documentary references to silver perfume-burners under the name of 'fumitories' occurred in the early 16th century and they almost certainly existed before. They were always confined to the houses of the wealthy even in the reign of Charles II (1660–1685) and the earliest surviving specimens are of this period, when they were first called cassolets. They consisted of low braziers with richly pierced covers and their function was to disguise the stenches which contemporary standards of hygiene rendered inevitable. Even ladies were not much given to washing, and the diarist Anthony à Wood recorded that courtiers at Whitehall Palace were in the habit of relieving nature in the fireplaces.

Caster: a comparatively narrow vessel for shaking pepper or other spices and later, sugar, over food through a perforated cover. The earliest surviving examples date from the second half of the 16th century and are exceedingly rare. They might be either vase-shaped and free-standing, or consist of small, detachable receptacles in the tops of bell-salts. Many more of the independent kind are extant from 1660 onwards. These were often made in sets of three, one large – up to 22 cm high – and two smaller, though it is evident that they were sometimes supplied separately. It is probable that the large one was generally used for sugar and the smaller for various spices including cinnamon and pepper, but the owner of such objects would naturally tend to please himself as to the nature of the contents.

Until the early 18th century, their form was cylindrical and they were surmounted by tall, domed covers, decorated by hand with saw-cut patterns. These covers were attached by a slip-lock joint consisting of a pair of lugs, one opposite the other, each of which, when the cover was twisted round, came opposite a key-way in an encircling moulding so that the cover could be pulled off vertically. The earliest feet consisted of simple mouldings, but in the last decade of the 17th century they were commonly embellished with small gadroons, often alternating

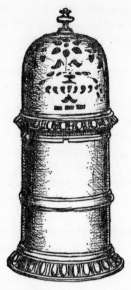

Caster, c. 1700

Caster, c. 1710

Caster, c. 1740

with flutes. This cylindrical type soon became outmoded after the succession of Queen Anne in 1702 and was followed by a baluster-shape which remained popular up to about 1720 in connection with large casters, but thereafter its incidence declined steeply and the shape was generally confined to small casters until about 1750. The latter usually had covers in the form of a low dome, often finished with a knob or a pointed finial and looking something like a German *Pickel-haube* helmet of the time of Kaiser Wilhelm II. The covers of these smaller casters were of simple pull-off type, and the same system was soon extended to the larger variants, so that the slip-lock joint almost disappeared. Apart from a true baluster of architectural type, an inverted baluster was also used as a source of inspiration on occasions. Both kinds were liable to be decorated with cut-card work (q.v.).

Meanwhile, another shape had appeared in the first decade of the century, and this was destined to be exceedingly popular in the reign of George II (1727–1760), when a London silversmith named Samuel Wood specialised in the manufacture of casters. Apart from the usual highly-domed cover, the body was of a shape strongly reminiscent of the cup-turning often found on legged furniture of the late 17th century. A moulding encircled it at its largest diameter in the lower third and above this, the sides made a concave curve, then rose vertically. Smaller casters were often of similar shape as an alternative to the baluster, especially when they formed part of a set of three. All these various casters of the first half of the 18th century might be of either polygonal or circular section, the latter being more frequent. Before pursuing the main line of development further, mention must be made of another kind of caster, commonly known by the modern jargon phrase, 'kitchen pepper', though it seems unlikely that it would ever have been entrusted to the mercies of a cook. It was cylindrical and provided with a single scrolled handle like that of a mug. The type belonged in general to the early 18th century, though it persisted rather longer in Ireland than in England.

From about the middle of the 18th century, many casters had bodies of the same swag-bellied form found on other contemporary objects. Below the widest part of the protuberance the outline curved inward, then changed direction and drooped downward to the rounded base above the foot-ring. The shape cannot be considered an improvement on any of those which preceded it, and although it was characteristic of the rococo (q.v.) period, when it was occasionally embossed with appropriate ornament, it continued into the neo-classical phase associated with the name of Robert Adam (q.v.). The casters of the latter period were poor compared with other contemporary objects. Some were like small urns, but many had cylindrical bodies mounted on short stems and feet, with a pierced pyramidal cover extending beyond the sides and looking like a Chinese hat. These continued to be made in the early 19th century, when designers had little new to offer in this connection. *See* 'Kitchen pepper'.

Cast work: this was used from ancient times for ornamentation, but actual objects including hollowware were sometimes produced by this means on rare occasions, even in the 18th and 19th centuries. Two main methods were employed. For fine detail or objects of high quality the *cire perdue* (lost wax) process was employed as in the case of metal statuary. The following is a simplified account of the process. First, a rough form was made of a refractory substance such as a mixture of clay or sand. Wax was spread over this and was modelled with tools to the degree of finish required in the casting. This was then covered with a 'mother shell' of damp clay, the interior of which took a negative impression of the wax surface. When the whole was heated, the wax melted and ran out of vents provided for the purpose. The space which it had previously occupied was then filled with molten silver, which received from the inside of the mother shell the shape and surface details of the original wax model, of which it necessarily formed an exact replica. The core was then broken out and any excrescences formed by the vents filed off. Where necessary, finish was improved with hand tools. For small objects, the model was made entirely of wax without a core, so that the resultant casting was solid. The other chief method was to make the castings in an ordinary sand mould. They were often carelessly finished and with pock-marked surfaces. It is evident that this process was sometimes used to make such small items as the cast figure-finials on the covers of certain salts and standing cups of the 16th century.

Caudle cup: a name sometimes applied, without any certainty of correctness, to large covered two-handled cups of the 17th century, especially those with ogee-shaped bodies. As there is no evidence to support the usage it must be regarded as undesirable. Caudle was thin gruel mixed with spiced wine or ale, sugar and spices.

Censer, or Thurible: a container with an open-work superstructure used for burning incense in religious ceremonies. The censer was swung on chains to provide a draught and spread the aromatic smoke. English silver examples have survived from the 14th century, though many others in the Gothic style were doubtless destroyed after the Reformation.

Centrepiece: a more desirable term for what is otherwise known by the bogus French word *épergne* (q.v.), though the latter has attained respectability in Great Britain through long usage; in France, it has never been used at all. Centrepieces were known in the early 18th century and have always embodied a varying number of requisites. These might include table baskets, salts, candle-holders, casters, sauce-boats, waiters and sweetmeat baskets which were suspended from or attached to branching arms. Some of the more elaborate examples had interchangeable fittings as they could not all be used at once, and if any of the branches were not required they could be removed, the vacant sockets having decorative silver knobs inserted so that the centrepiece looked complete. Some of the earliest survivors are from the second quarter of the 18th century during the rococo (q.v.) period, some of them including much heavy, cast detail and ornamental engraving, often of very high quality. The centrepieces of the Adam (q.v.) period were so decorated with piercing that they generally had a somewhat mean and spidery appearance. Those of the early 19th century often had a dignified and monumental aspect which was greatly in keeping with the ostentation inherent in the character of the objects concerned.

Chalice: a wine-cup for administering Holy Communion. In the early days of the Church in England and Ireland, when the sacrament was given to the laity in both kinds, chalices were sometimes large bowl-like objects equipped with two handles, but after the Norman conquest, generally assumed the more familiar form of a goblet with stem and foot. For several centuries, secular standing cups and ecclesiastical chalices were more or less identical and even in the 15th century, lay benefactors sometimes donated their domestic drinking cups to churches. In the 11th century, the bowl of a chalice was wide, shallow and rather less than a hemisphere, while the stem spread downward in the shape of a trumpet to form a foot. A plain or decorated knop (or 'knot' as it was called in the middle ages) was positioned a short distance below the base of the bowl. In the 13th century, a change occurred in the stem, which remained of practically the same diameter until just above the foot, so that instead of the two parts merging together they became more distinct. This type continued to be made in the 14th century, but was eventually superseded by a chalice with a rounder and deeper bowl and a cylindrical or polygonal stem of columnar appearance. The wide knop, often decorated with angels' heads or ornament reminiscent of the kind found on roof-bosses, was set more or less in the centre of the stem. The foot was usually hollow-cusped, that is, it projected in a

Chalice, 15th century

number of concave-sided points. This type of chalice continued with little modification through the 15th century, but after 1500, the cusps were often replaced by convex lobes. As the Church, unlike secular owners of plate, was little affected by changes in fashion, many old chalices in the Gothic style continued in use after the Reformation. They were supremely suitable for their purpose, and their traditional design emphasised the timeless continuity of the Christian faith, so that no one had any desire to replace them. In the reign of Elizabeth I (1558–1603) however, orders were issued by the Anglican bishops to their parish priests requiring them to destroy their chalices and provide 'decent communion cups' in their room. As a result of this piece of puerile bigotry, most of the beautiful English medieval chalices were consigned to the crucible and were replaced by a greatly inferior type of standing beaker, which had occurred sparsely since about 1550. Technically, it could be said that the chalice ceased to exist as an element of the English liturgy at this time except among recusants, who risked the penal laws to maintain their ritual in secret. But the difference is more terminological than real, and the 'decent communion cup', however dull and bathetic, was merely a degenerate lineal descendant of the chalice. In the 17th century, the decline became more marked. The tall bowls developed rounded bases and the generally unknopped stems were of trumpet-shape; this type persisted into the 18th century despite its inconvenience. Later, when the prejudice against the trappings of the Roman Church had subsided, some Anglican churches obtained communion cups of a very chalice-like aspect and in a modified Gothic design, and many of these are still in use. Until the second half of the 16th century, most chalices were wholly or partly gilt.

Chamber candlestick, c. 1760

Chamber candlestick: a low candlestick with a wide pan forming the base, and a scroll or loop handle fixed to the edge. There are virtually no survivors from before the late 17th century and they were rare until after 1700. The commonest 18th-century type had a short, baluster-shaped socket, and either this or the inner part of the handle had an attached projection with a vertical aperture into which a corresponding prong on the extinguisher fitted. These extinguishers, which were found more convenient than douters (q.v.), were conical, usually with a small knob finial. Snuffers (q.v.) were usually provided with their own tray or stand, but in the second half of the 18th century, often accompanied the chamber candlestick, lying across the pan and passing through a wide slot in the lower part of the socket. Some of the pans were raised on three short feet, others rested on their own bases. Ornament, when present, followed the prevailing mode, but many were quite plain until the early 19th century, when they tended to assume a massive appearance in accordance with contemporary taste.

Chamber-pot, c. 1660

Chamber-pot: silver chamber-pots were in use at the end of the 16th century, but none has endured from before the second half of the 17th century. Examples from the Georgian period are rather less infrequently encountered, but all are very rare, probably because silver was seldom used for the purpose. The few survivors are similar to their counterparts in pewter, with comparatively narrow, bulbous bodies with everted, flattened rims for the comfort of female users. A single handle, like that of a mug, was fixed to one side. Unconvincing attempts have occasionally been made to convert them into punch-bowls by removing the handle.

Chandelier: a hanging, branched candlestick with multiple sockets. Silver examples were always rare in England but were known in the first half of the 16th century and possibly before, when they may have followed the design of contemporary wooden candle-beams. The few survivors were made during the century following the restoration of the Monarchy in 1660. A fine specimen, made for William III, is at Hampton Court Palace, two made in 1734 are in the Kremlin in Moscow, and the Fishmongers' Company of the City of London owns a seventeen-branched example, of 1752. None is known after this date, probably because cut-glass became more fashionable for the purpose.

Chasing: the decoration of plate with linear designs by means of a chaser. This instrument was a kind of punch with a blunt end like that of a small screwdriver. The top was struck with a hammer so that as the chaser was moved along, lines were formed by the compression of the metal. Chasing was used by itself, when it is often called flat-chasing, or in association with embossing (q.v.).

Cheese-scoop: a kind of long spoon, often with an ivory handle, having a bowl shaped like a half cylinder, and used for scooping cheese such as Stilton out of the interior; mostly late 18th and early 19th centuries.

Chester

Chester: workers in precious metal were active in the ancient city of Chester as early as the 10th century in connection with the minting of coins, but the first references to Goldsmiths occurred in the early 13th century. Although it seems evident that plate was made in the city throughout the middle ages, it was not until the last decade of the 17th century that assaying and marking began to be organised on a regular basis. Even then, date-letters were sometimes current for more than one year until 1701. From this year until 1779, the town mark consisted of the royal arms of England impaling the dimidiated arms of the city, but the city arms alone were used thereafter until August 1962 when the assay office ceased to operate.

Chinoiserie ornament, c. 1670

Chinoiserie: a name given to designs of a pseudo-Oriental character used in the decoration of plate from about 1660. They were commonly engraved or chased in the first phase, which lasted, with diminishing vigour, until the end of the 17th century. The Orient was so far away that no one was concerned with accuracy and the designs often included palm-trees with undulating trunks, large exotic birds and 'Chinamen' wearing Indian turbans. Chinoiserie returned to favour with the rococo (q.v.) style in the second quarter of the 18th century and affected plate no less than furniture, the ornament being frequently embossed. It was still by no means accurately Chinese, but some of the more obvious incongruities of the 17th century were excluded.

Chocolate-cup frame: a silver frame for holding a beaker-like porcelain cup, probably introduced in about 1715. It comprised a saucer, about 12 cm in diameter, with a detachable holder consisting of a circular base with four vertical scrolls supporting a ring. They seem to have been fairly numerous in the first half of the 18th century, but examples are now rare, possibly due to the fact that when chocolate declined in popularity, many of them were melted down.

Chocolate-pot: chocolate began to be drunk in England shortly after the middle of the 17th century, but the period of its greatest popularity was from about 1680 to 1730. The vessels used for serving the beverage were entirely similar to coffee-pots (q.v.) apart from one detail. This was a removable finial on the top of the lid which exposed a small aperture through which a rod was inserted to stir the contents immediately before pouring. This ensured that the skin which formed on the surface of the chocolate was shared out among the company instead of falling to the lot of a single unfortunate individual. The finials could be pulled out, twisted sideways, or swung back on a hinge. It is sometimes the practice to describe as chocolate-pots certain jug-like vessels of later periods with pouring-lips instead of spouts, but most of these could have served equally well for hot water or sometimes hot milk. Chocolate never enjoyed the same popularity in England as tea and coffee.

Ciborium: a goblet-like vessel with a cover, used to contain Communion wafers.

Wine-cistern, c. 1690

Cistern: wine-cisterns began to be made of silver after 1660, though examples in pewter and other non-precious metals were in use half a century before. Their purpose was to cool bottles or decanters of wine, which were stood in cold water in the cistern until they were required. Silver versions were almost invariably oval and were mounted on either bases or feet. They continued to be produced until the late 18th century and reflected all the changing styles which affected plate of all kinds. They were especially prevalent in the early 18th century and varied considerably in size. Some were comparatively small – about 50 cm long and 30 cm high – but others were enormous and were large enough to be used as baths with some degree of comfort. Among these may be mentioned a magnificent specimen at Penshurst Place in Kent, belonging to Lord de L'Isle and Dudley, and another by Charles Kandler of London which was eventually bought by the Empress Catherine II of Russia.

Coaster, c. 1810

Coaster: a short cylindrical holder for a decanter, usually with a turned wooden base covered underneath with baize and with silver sides. It enabled the decanter to be slid along the table without damaging the polished surface and also protected it against spilt liquor. The earliest examples of this type probably appeared during the neo-classical period (see Adam) and commonly had straight sides with pierced ornament like much other contempoary plate. These were intended to hold the tall tapering decanters of the period. In the early 19th century, ornament tended to become heavier like the coasters themselves. Fruiting vines and *amorini* were favourite motifs, some being embossed from the inside, others being cast and applied. At the same time, rococo decoration began to be revived, but usually appeared on coasters of a pronounced Regency (q.v.) character, with bulging sides and widely everted rims which were often boldly gadrooned. These more pon-derous-looking coasters were a fitting accompaniment to the heavy Prussian-shaped or cylindrical decanters, which were often profusely cut with relief diamonds and other designs. At the end of the 18th century, various kinds of stand for two decanters appeared. These were often equipped with wheels and were more typical of the early 19th century. *See* Bottle-stand.

Coco-nut cup: silver-mounted standing cups with bowls made from coco-nut shells are mentioned in 13th-century records, but the earliest survivors date from the late 14th century. Even more have remained from the 15th century, and these conform in many respects with the design of other vessels of the same period. Stems were trumpet-shaped, swelling out at the base into a circular foot. This was often embellished with a common form of Gothic architectural ornament consisting of a gallery with vertical hollow cusps, each terminating in a formalised flower-head. The silver lip-band of the cup was connected to the top of the stem by several vertical silver straps with ornamental edges. These straps were necessary to hold the cup together, as the stem could naturally not be soldered on to the base of the coco-nut shell. The same technique was used in connection with ostrich-egg cups (q.v.). When the renaissance style superseded the Gothic in the first half of the 16th century, the silver portions of coco-nut cups were similar to those on other contemporary vessels (*see* Cups, standing). Silver-mounted coco-nut cups ceased to enjoy fashionable esteem in about the middle of the 17th century, though occasional examples, often unmarked, appeared from time to time even in the 18th century.

Coffee-pot: although coffee-houses were opened in increasing numbers from the middle of the 17th century onwards, the earliest known silver coffee-pot is the example of 1681 in the Victoria & Albert Museum, London. The body is in the form of a tall, upward-tapering cylinder, with a straight spout and a hinged lid in the shape of a cone. The scrolled handle of this and other early specimens is of the kind found on tankards, and is wrought from sheet silver of a hollow D-section. For insulation, the handle is bound with leather. The same shape persisted for a while after 1700, but in the last decade of the 17th century, handles began to be made of a hard South-American wood or

Coffee-pot, c. 1680

Coffee-pot, c. 1705

Coffee-pot, c. 1760

Coffee-pot, c. 1775

ivory and were often set at right-angles to the spout. The latter showed an increasing tendency towards curvature and was sometimes provided with a hinged cap to retain the heat, but the fully-developed swan-necked spout did not appear until the turn of the century. At the same

61

time, lids generally assumed the high domed formation found also on contemporary tea-pots (q.v.), but by 1720, the dome had become lower, and bodies were often of a very attractive polygonal section. A quasi-baluster shape had already made an appearance in coffee-pots (and chocolate-pots) quite early in the century, but although the true baluster was also known, it did not become widely prevalent until about 1750. It continued to be used for the remainder of the 18th century despite the introduction of other shapes. Among the latter may be mentioned a rather unfortunate swag-bellied form, which occurred in other contemporary hollowware during the currency of the rococo (q.v.) style, and the designs of the Adam (q.v.) period deriving from classical urns. The urn-shape continued after 1800, with a shorter stem than previously and a more rounded base to the receptacle, but more typical of the Regency (q.v.) period was a jug-like coffee-pot with bulging base, mounted on either a foot-ring or legs and with a tongue-like pouring-lip jutting out at the top.

Coffee-spoon: no special sort of spoon seems to have been made for coffee before the 20th century. *See* Spoon, tea.

Coffee-urn: the larger urns, common from about 1760 onwards, were used to contain hot water for tea, but a few coffee-urns were made in the early 18th century. These were of two kinds, both deriving from Continental prototypes. One was shaped like an ordinary coffee-pot, but had a tap at the base instead of a spout and was mounted on a stand. The other looked like a small wine-fountain (q.v.) and was shaped like a 'Borghese' urn, with a gadrooned protuberance at the bottom bearing a tap above the wide stem. It is possible that this variety was, in fact, simply a small wine-fountain, though there is no doubt that it was used as a coffee-urn in the Netherlands. Both kinds were exceedingly rare in England, where ordinary coffee-pots were manifestly preferred.

College cup: a type of two-handled cup for drinking, so called because some are known to have been in use at Cambridge University before the Civil War, and a few are still preserved at various Oxford colleges and at Eton. Their use, however, was probably more general than the name suggests, as it has never been a feature of English silver-smithing for certain vessels to be confined to particular environments. They had baluster-shaped bodies, stout, expansive foot-rings, and a pair of small circular handles soldered to opposite sides of the neck. The type was exclusively 17th-century and the earliest of surviving examples made in 1616 is in the possession of the Mercers' Company of the City of London. *See* Cup, two-handled.

Communion cup: the successor after the Reformation of the ecclesi-astical chalice (q.v.).

Convoys: an old name for base or sub-standard metal added to a piece of plate in such a manner as to make detection difficult, with the fraudulent object of increasing the apparent weight of precious metal.

Cork: it is known that silversmiths were working in Cork at least as early as the 15th century, and that they were co-members of a guild embracing craftsmen of other kinds from 1656. Although several attempts were made during the 18th and early 19th centuries to establish an assay office they were always frustrated, largely owing to the oppo-sition of the Dublin guild. There is no doubt however that consider-able quantities of plate were produced in the city at least up to the first quarter of the 19th century, but the fact that the guild including the plate-workers had ceased to exist by 1850, suggests a diminution of activity after about 1820. It appears that purchasers of Cork plate generally had a justified confidence in the integrity of the silversmiths and were content to accept the maker's mark as a guarantee of quality. Date-letters were never used, so Cork plate can be assigned to its period only on stylistic grounds and the evidence afforded by the makers' marks. Large numbers of these from 1662 to 1838 are listed in Sir Charles Jackson's *English Goldsmiths and Their Marks*. As there was never any legal sanction for the various marks which were applied, they . were presumably subject only to local arrangements among the con-fraternity; nevertheless, proper standards were maintained as a matter of self-respect. Town marks varied, and included a ship and a castle, while the words 'Sterling', spelt in various ways, and 'Dollar' (which showed that the origin of the metal was captured Spanish crown-pieces) indicated the standard at different times. Despite the rather chaotic character of the marking system, Cork plate was as good as any other.

Cream-boat: an 18th-century utensil for serving cream, usually in connection with tea, shaped like a small sauce-boat (q.v.) on short legs; especially prevalent in Scotland as an alternative to a cream-jug.

Cream-jug: *see* Jug, cream or milk.

Cruet-frame: a silver stand to contain glass cruets in rings or sockets, for vinegar, oil, etc. These frames may have appeared first in the late 17th century, when the use of silver was constantly spreading, but the earliest examples known date from about 1710. Simpler variants held no more than two silver-mounted glass cruets shaped rather like miniature decanters, but others, now often known as 'Warwick frames', contained three silver casters (q.v.) as well, one large and two small. This popular design continued through the rococo (q.v.) phase, often with an applied asymmetrical cartouche for the owner's arms, crest or monogram. In the Adam (q.v.) period, treatment tended to become flimsier, but a new type appeared with sides of pierced sheet silver, often of oval shape and looking somewhat like an enlarged version of a certain kind of contemporary salt (q.v.). Others were simply oval platforms supporting retaining rings. In the early 19th century, the same basic principles conditioned the design of many frames but in the Regency (q.v.) idiom. There was still a noticeable affinity with contemporary salts, but the overall shape was usually rounded-oblong and the sheet-silver sides had an outward bulge.

Cup: a generic term for a silver drinking vessel of any kind, often occurring in combinations such as two-handled cup, standing cup and even tankard cup. *See* under separate headings, e.g. Cup, standing.

Cup, Magdalen: *see* Beaker.

Standing cup, c. 1450

Cup, standing: a covered or uncovered drinking vessel, either of silver or a non-metallic substance with silver mounts, consisting of a bowl of varied shape supported on a stem and foot. Throughout their long history, these vessels were made in a wide range of sizes, the smaller, uncovered versions being now usually known as wine-cups.

Silver standing cups existed in Anglo-Saxon England, as is attested by a 9th-century example in the British Museum, but survivors are more frequent from the Gothic (q.v.) period. A sole remaining specimen from just after the middle of the 12th century, made of low-standard silver, was discovered in 1890 in the stone coffin of Archbishop Hubert Walter in Canterbury Cathedral. This was evidently an ecclesiastical chalice, but secular vessels must have been of identical type, for a very similar cup is illustrated in an 11th-century manuscript showing a festive board. The trumpet-shaped stem broadens out into a circular foot and a knop – or 'knot' as it was called in the middle ages – is situated just below the wide, shallow bowl. Although the same kind of bowl persisted through the 13th century and well into the century following, the stem became cylindrical after 1200 and the knop was positioned more centrally. Cups of this design also were used us chalices, though these were never provided with permanent covers like many of their secular counterparts of all periods.

In 14th-century documents there are references to a type of vessel called a 'hanap'. It seems evident, from the usual nature of the context, that the term denoted a large standing cup of important aspect with a cover. A number of silver drinking vessels given to Edward, Prince of Wales in 1371 included 'one gilded hanap in the form of an acorn', though we have to wait a further two centuries for surviving examples of acorn cups.

It is possible that standing cups which derived their shape from the beaker (q.v.) first began to occur in England in the 14th century, but the only known remaining specimen of the period is the so-called King John Cup owned by the Corporation of King's Lynn, Norfolk. The name is purely fanciful, and although it probably enshrines some ancient, forgotten tradition, the bowl and foot are decorated in enamel with figures in the costume of the 14th century, when it was undoubtedly made.

A reference to a coco-nut cup occurred in the middle of the 13th century, but the earliest known survivors are of late 14th- or early 15th-century origin. Even more have endured from later in the latter century, and the designs are all basically similar. The stem of each is of upward-tapering trumpet-shape, the polished shell has a slice cut off the top to convert it into a usable cup, and the rim has a silver band connected to the top of the stem by decorated vertical straps of the same metal. Trumpet-shaped stems of varying length were also found from the early 15th century on standing cups made wholly of silver. Their bowls were generally narrower and deeper than those of the previous century, and they were frequently decorated with Gothic ornament in the form of an applied gallery round the base of the stem and, where appropriate, the edge of the cover. This gallery consisted of a circuit of small hollow-sided cusps, each apex being crowned by a conventionalised flower-head. Similar ornament was often found on coco-nut cups and standing mazers (q.v.) and persisted, together with the trumpet stem, until the Gothic style began to be superseded by that of the renaissance in the first half of the 16th century.

In about 1500 appeared the font-shaped cup. This had a short trumpet stem of the kind often found in the 15th century, but the sides of the wide, shallow bowl were straight instead of curved. A related type was simply known as a flat cup. This had a taller stem and the bowl was turned out slightly at the top. As the renaissance style gained ground a new repertoire of ornament came into use and included gadroons, acanthus leaves (q.q.v.), and scroll brackets. Stems were often in the form of vases or urns, and so frequently were these elements used as a source of inspiration that these parts of standing cups became known as 'potkins'. A new type of bowl was also introduced and was derived, with some modification of proportion, from a kind of late classical urn with a protuberance at the base which gave it something of the appearance of a thistle.

Font-shaped cup, c. 1500

From about the middle of the 16th century, parts of silver objects of all kinds were often embossed with small, lumpy fruits and engraved strapwork (q.v.), which, together with scrollwork, continued into the early 17th century. Contemporary with the thistle-shaped cup were others whose bowls were made from coco-nuts, ostrich eggs, nautilus shells and rock crystal, the silver or silver-gilt mounts all being similar. For many years it was supposed that crystal had the power of detecting poison.

In the second half of the century, while English plate was still under noticeable German influence, various fanciful designs came to England from the Habsburg empire, though their incidence was never very high. These included bowls shaped like gourds and melons, the curved portion at the top being completed by the cover. Acorn cups were also made, though these had already been known since the 14th century. The stems of all these usually derived their form as far as possible from

Standing cup, c. 1550   *Standing cup, c. 1580*

that of the plant in question, and their production extended into the early 17th century.

New styles always overlapped those already in existence, and for many years the latter continued alongside designs displaying a greater degree of simplicity. This represented a growing reaction against the plethoric nature of German ornament and involved a stronger emphasis on form and proportion as opposed to decoration. Bowls, which were frequently shaped in profile like a catenary curve and varied in height and width, were seldom embellished with anything but linear engraving, while stems usually consisted of little more than miniature inverted architectural balusters. Covers, when they occurred, were mostly low domes surmounted by simple turned finials.

Apart from the more monumental covered cups, the last quarter of the 16th century saw the introduction and widespread acceptance of small wine-cups without covers. These had funnel-shaped bowls with rounded bases conceived on an altogether more modest scale, and the stems consisted of slim variants of the inverted baluster. They were cheaper than larger vessels and remained popular up to about the middle of the 17th century, evolving in accordance with the various contemporary influences.

Steeple cup, c. 1610

At the very end of the 16th century a totally new feature appeared. This was the steeple finial on the covers which was highly typical of the reign of Elizabeth's successor, James I (1603–1625). It was usually of triangular section and might be in sheet metal or openwork. Occasionally, it stood on a low collet, but was commonly supported on three small scroll brackets, one at each angle. The accompanying stems were also of a different character and comprised an elaborate inverted baluster, with two protuberances instead of one, with applied scroll brackets which added to the interest of the outline. The foot narrowed upward to the base of the baluster in the shape of a hollow-sided cone with rounded apex, the upper part virtually constituting part of the stem. The earliest bowls were of ovoid shape but soon became somewhat blunter at the base. Steeple cups had become generally obsolete by 1640 and the outbreak of the Civil War shortly after not only brought about a swingeing reduction in the manufacture of plate, but also caused the wholesale destruction of vast quantities already in existence, to provide bullion for conversion into coin. One type of wine-cup, however, which had first appeared in the reign of Charles I (1625–1649) continued to be manufactured to a slight extent during the interregnum, when England was ruled by Cromwell's military dictatorship. Its stem-formation represented a continuance of the taste of the late 16th century and consisted of a simple, robust inverted baluster; the bowl, however, was shaped somewhat like a bucket and was

Wine-cup, c. 1640

evidently inspired by the beaker (q.v.). These unostentatious but well-proportioned standing cups were never decorated and were in white silver. Ever since the early middle ages, all plate of any importance had been wholly or partly (parcel) gilt, but from the first quarter of the 17th century, gilding became exceptional.

By the time of the Restoration in 1660, standing cups had largely fallen out of fashion, because of the economic stringency of the Commonwealth period and the temporary eclipse of luxury trades in general. A few of the more monumental sort continued nevertheless to be made in the reign of Charles II and later, with stems of varying height and elaboration which almost invariably included an inverted baluster accompanied by subsidiary mouldings. Covers were sometimes surmounted by a descendant of the earlier steeple finial which was conceived in a totally different manner. It was of circular section and an integral part of the cover, from which it was drawn upward instead of being made separately and applied. Silver cups with stems and feet were no longer in general use in domestic surroundings, partly owing to the competition of the classically-inspired two-handled cup (*see* Cup, two-handled), partly because the nation had been developing a growing taste for drinking glasses, and the few that were made were mostly for ceremonial use by such bodies as colleges of universities and City livery companies. An example presented by Samuel Pepys to the Clothworkers' Company was decorated by means of a rare technique which was usually confined to two-handled cups. This involved the enclosing of the bowl in a pierced and chased outer casing which permitted the gilt underlying surface to show through the interstices.

Goblet, c. 1780

Goblet, c. 1810

A few official standing cups appeared from time to time in the first half of the 18th century, but with the dawn of the neo-classical period (see Adam), genuinely functional stemmed goblets came once more into use despite the flourishing state of the glass industry. These cups derived with some fidelity from classical originals. Their bowls were ovoid, their short stems were more or less cylindrical and their feet were chiefly circular or square. As in the case of glass rummers, the bowls dominated the design. The most popular type had a capacity slightly less than half a pint. These goblets persisted into the 19th century, but the new Regency style brought in a different bowl with a protuberance at the base which derived from a later and more robust form of classical urn and constituted, in modified form, a return to the thistle shape of the early 16th century. The basal protuberance was often boldly gadrooned and there was a fondness for cast and applied fruiting vines in the upper part. With the waning of the Regency style, functional silver standing cups virtually disappeared.

Cup, two-handled: the distant prototype of all English two-handled cups was the ancient Greek *kantharos*. This occurs in various forms on carvings and so forth of the classical era, some examples being like urns with stems and feet and often very large. It is evident, from the many instances in which the *kantharos* is shown in use, that it was primarily or exclusively a drinking vessel. The eclectic Roman civilisation has yielded related examples in different materials such as glass and silver, and it was probably from this source that a later, simpler variety developed in Italy. This type is exemplified by a 12th-century specimen, made of rock crystal with silver mounts, preserved in the treasury of St Mark's, Venice. Instead of being mounted on a stem and foot like the commonest form of the *kantharos*, its wide, U-shaped bowl is supported on a silver foot-ring placed almost immediately beneath its base. Many later two-handled cups for secular use either conformed to one or other of these basic designs or were hybrids of both, as will be seen later.

Large, two-handled vessels of silver or base metal are often shown in English medieval manuscripts standing on 'cup boards' together with beakers and standing cups, but they were known as 'livery pots' (q.v.) and were intended for serving liquor, not for drinking it. Two-handled drinking cups did not appear on the English domestic scene until the early 16th century, at a time when renaissance influence was beginning to replace the Gothic. This influence, which emanated from Italy, reached England chiefly *via* the Habsburg empire and its appanage, the Duchy of Burgundy. King Henry VIII was on terms of warm friendship with the Emperor Maximilian I who even served under his command at the siege of Thérouanne in 1513, and the arrival in England of the Augsburg artist Hans Holbein in 1526 no doubt gave a further impetus to the new style which was slowly beginning to find favour. In addition to being a distinguished painter Holbein was also a designer of weapons and silverware. In view of the channel by which the renaissance style arrived it is not surprising that English plate in general should have had a noticeable Germanic flavour for much of the 16th century.

Two-handled cup, c. 1530

College cup, c. 1620

Survivals from this early period are exceedingly rare, but two-handled cups must, in fact, have existed in fairly large numbers. This is evident from a 16th-century colloquial expression 'to make the pot with the two ears', which meant to set the arms akimbo. Expressions of this sort do not gain currency unless they refer to something which is familiar to a great many people. At this period, any vessel with a handle or handles, apart from a porringer (q.v.), was called a pot irrespective of its size. These early 'pots' or two-handled cups had an ogee-shaped outline, narrow above and bulbous below, so that their form was like that of a squat architectural baluster. References sometimes occur in contemporary documents to 'haunch pots' and it seems likely that this phrase denoted 'pots' of the kind under discussion, as their swelling form is reminiscent of the human pelvic region. The same fact helps to explain the colloquial expression for setting the arms akimbo, mentioned above. There was some variation in size and some variation in

73

height in relation to width, and these considerations applied also to a descendant of the type which was found in the early 17th century. This is generally known as a 'college cup' because examples are preserved in various university colleges and at Eton. Though entirely undecorated, it was of the same general shape as its precursors, but the handles consisted of two vertical rings, soldered to opposite sides of the neck and looking something like a pair of spectacles. It is not known whether the use of this kind of cup was confined to colleges, but it seems improbable. Any others which may have existed were no doubt melted down during the Civil War: a fate which befell vast quantities of plate of all kinds at the same time.

Late in the second quarter of the 17th century, when the Civil War had reduced silversmithing activity to a low ebb, appeared a modified version of the foregoing which was destined to be very popular after the restoration of the Monarchy in 1660. The body became wide and

Two-handled cup, c. 1645

Two-handled cup, c. 1655

short, it was often equipped with a cover, like numerous standing cups before it, and the cast handles were usually in the form of S-scrolls embodying bare-breasted female terminal figures, borrowed from the wide repertoire of renaissance ornament. This type continued into the late 17th century, but in the late 1650s it began to be challenged by a species of cup which was an apparent relative of the medieval example in Venice, made of crystal with silver mounts. The body was shaped like a wash-tub, wide at the rim and sloping gently inward towards the base, with handles of the terminal-figure variety. The commonest decoration comprised chased circles with punched ancillary ornament outside them and it cannot be pretended that the effect was anything but crude. Post-restoration examples of the same general shape were far more graceful and refined, as will be seen later.

The same period saw the introduction of the salver (q.v.) and this new piece of plate was sometimes accompanied by a covered two-handled cup, decorated *en suite* and clearly designed to form a garniture. As the salver was intended for use when 'giving beer or other liquid thing' it is evident that the accompanying two-handled cup was meant to contain such fluids.

The restoration of the Monarchy in 1660 ushered in a boom period for English silversmiths, due, no doubt, partly to a general desire to replace the enormous quantities of wrought silver converted into coin for payment of both armies during the Civil War, partly to satisfy an urge for a more luxurious mode of living. Although domestic standing cups ceased to be fashionable owing to the increasing competition from drinking glasses, the manufacture of two-handled cups reached unprecedented heights and helped to replace them. The type with the ogee-shaped profile continued and was frequently embossed with the florid botanical ornament of Dutch origin found on other plate at the same time. Large cups of this kind are often described as 'caudle cups' or 'posset pots', though there is, in fact, no evidence to support the notion that they were intended primarily to contain these semi-liquid foods, which were prepared by mixing gruel or milk with spiced wine or ale. The fact that they were sometimes accompanied by salvers indicates, on the contrary, that they were used chiefly for 'beer or other liquid thing' as mentioned previously.

More numerous than these were cups shaped more or less like a wide letter U, like the crystal specimen in Venice, many of them being made without covers. Some were plain, others were chased or engraved all over with the contemporary pseudo-Oriental ornament known as 'chinoiserie' (q.v.). But the most popular ornament, and certainly the most aesthetically satisfying, consisted of an embossed and chased circuit of alternate acanthus and palmette leaves, rising vertically from the base of the bowl and terminating at a varying distance below the middle. This treatment, which occurred on other kinds of hollowware also, struck an admirable balance between plain and decorated surfaces so that each enhanced the other.

It is in relation to these and later objects in the same category, either plain or decorated, that the incorrect name 'porringer' (q.v.) has been applied in Great Britain through popular ignorance. The term is demonstrably false and two examples are given to prove it. It should be noted that the word 'porridge' is a variant of 'pottage'.

(*a*) A portrait by Benedetto Gennari, painted in the reign of Charles II, shows Elizabeth Felton in the guise of Cleopatra, but in contemporary costume, acting out the well-known incident in which the Egyptian Queen dissolved a pearl in her wine in the presence of Mark Antony. The pearl is held in her left hand, while in her right is a silver two-handled cup with acanthus-leaf decoration of the kind mentioned above. It is clear from this beyond the smallest doubt that the type of cup depicted must have been recognised at the time as a normal drinking vessel and not as a utensil for food. (*See* frontispiece).

Two-handled cup, c. 1660   *Two-handled cup, c. 1670*

(*b*) A salver and accompanying two-handled cup of the Charles-II period were presented later to Colerne church in Wiltshire. The salver is inscribed: 'This Salver and Cup belonging was given for the use of the Sacrament...' It is quite evident, not only that a vessel for porridge or stew would not have been donated for the purpose described, but also that it would not have been referred to as a cup if it had been a porringer.

In Italy, these cups are known as *tazze a due manici* (two-handled cups) and Great Britain is, in fact, the only country in Europe in which they are miscalled 'porringers'. It is surely high time that this absurd usage was abandoned by all concerned, including dealers and auctioneers who ought to know better. It is a most unhappy state of affairs that influential members of these categories should often render fresh research nugatory by the tenacity with which they cling to various myths.

One form of decorative technique should be mentioned before we consider two-handled cups of the next stylistic phase. This consisted of enclosing the bowl and cover in an embossed outer sleeve which was pierced between the motifs so that the gilded underlying surface showed through. Most two-handled cups treated in this manner had cylindrical bodies, presumably to minimise technical problems, but a few were of the normal curved shape. The ornament was generally of a Dutch character and might include flowers, scrolling foliage and exotic birds such as turkeys.

Two-handled cup, c. 1680

Two-handled cups of the Charles-II period with acanthus decoration are probably the most pleasing ever produced, but the style did not generally survive beyond 1690.

In the last decade of the 17th century we note the advent of what is usually known as the 'Queen Anne style'. The phrase is inaccurate but there is no harm in it provided one remembers that the style so described began well before Anne's accession in 1702 and continued for many years after her death in 1714. In connection with two-handled cups it often manifested itself in the form of spiralled gadroons alternating with flutes round the lower parts of the bodies and frequently, though not invariably, with an embossed cable-moulding a short distance below the rim. Simple scroll handles had been competing with the terminal-figure versions since the reign of Charles II and were now almost the only type used apart from a notable exception which will be mentioned later. Foot-rings were absent from these functional domestic vessels except in a minute number of instances, so that they rested on the actual base of the bowl, which was accordingly unprotected from wear. This has often resulted in cracking round the edge, especially with the many examples made of silver of the Britannia standard (q.v.)

Two-handled cup, c. 1700

which was compulsory between 1697 and 1720. The vast majority were without covers. These honest but rather humble cups continued to be made for ordinary household use until the second half of the century, but growing narrower in relation to their height. The proportions of these later examples were less pleasing.

Meanwhile, two-handled cups of a more monumental character had been made since the late 17th century and increased in incidence as the 18th century advanced. Their popularisation was almost certainly due to immigrant French Huguenot silversmiths who had eventually found refuge in England and Ireland to escape the persecutions attendant upon the revocation of the Edict of Nantes by Louis XIV. These resourceful craftsmen were able to establish wealthy clienteles partly, no doubt, on account of the xenophilia often found at many periods among men and women of fashion, partly because their work was of a very high standard. As a matter of commercial policy they naturally deemed it expedient to draw attention to themselves as much as possible, and since advertising as we understand it now was then crude and naïve, their only course was to give their productions a distinctive character. This they achieved in the spheres of both decoration and form. Decoration often involved the use of cast and applied ornament, cut-card work and fluting and gadrooning of a highly-finished order. Both cast and cut-card work (q.v.) added notably to the cost of a piece by necessitating the use of extra precious metal, but for the clients whom the Huguenots

Two-handled cup, c. 1710

hoped to interest, the expensive nature of the finished product was probably an added inducement to possess it. In regard to form, the emphasis was on curvaceousness, so that the rather dumpy shape of the ordinary domestic cup was avoided and bodies turned further inward at the base and rested on foot-rings. The constriction between the bottom of the actual receptacle and the foot-ring soon developed into a stem: rudimentary at first but increasing in height with the passage of time, so that the general conception began to approximate to that of the Greek *kantharos*. Harp-shaped handles, popular in France at the same time, often supplied an alternative to the usual scrolls. English silversmiths soon began to adopt the same methods until the styles of the two nationalities eventually fused. Two-handled cups of the more important kind thus took on an imposing aspect which made them seem like objects of art rather than objects of use and there is no doubt that the achievement of higher theoretical aesthetic standards was made at the expense of a certain amount of sincerity. They were, of course, still usable as drinking vessels and probably figured in loving-cup ceremonies, but it seems likely that the larger specimens spent most of their time standing on furniture or chimney-pieces in a purely decorative role.

Two-handled cup, c. 1780

Rococo (q.v.) ornament began to be applied in the second quarter of the 18th century and remained popular until about 1770, sometimes accompanied by a body of swag-bellied shape. The base began to curve inward then suddenly drooped downward, before finally curving in to the bottom, producing a singularly unattractive outline. The same form occurred on other contemporary objects and persisted well after 1760, but two-handled cups of orthodox profile were made as well and were probably more numerous.

When rococo was generally superseded by the neo-classical style in about 1770, due mainly to the exertions of Robert Adam (q.v.), the classical urn provided silversmiths with a ready-made pattern for two-handled cups. The basic form was like that of a common china egg-cup, but with the addition of vertical loop-handles and usually a cover. Some were quite plain, like much other plate of all periods, but most were decorated with typical neo-classical motifs of the kind found in architecture, furniture etc., at the same time. Their aspect was monumental, though more graceful than their predecessors, and the larger varieties took on the status of vases. They were, however, still considered as belonging to the category of drinking vessels and a number were made as prize cups for horse-races. These urn-like cups were produced until shortly after 1800, when they were ousted from popular esteem by similar objects conceived in the newly emergent Regency style (q.v.).

This style laid great emphasis on massiveness, in accordance with the views of professional designers such as the architect Charles Heathcote Tatham. This quality manifested itself in cups inspired by heavy, late classical originals which had been known to the designers of the late 18th century but had been eschewed owing to their ponderous inelegance. The administrators of Lloyd's Patriotic Fund (q.v.) commissioned a large number of heavy cups with vertical handles curling inward at the top like fern-shoots.

Of more general application was a design based on that of a late classical urn with a protuberance at the base of the body which gave it something of the appearance of a thistle: a shape sometimes known as the 'Borghese urn'. The handles of these cups consisted most frequently of short, horizontal loops, often finely reeded, while the upper parts of the bodies might be embellished with applied fruiting vines, rendered with much fidelity but liable to harbour all kinds of foreign matter under the edges of their projecting leaves.

It is difficult to believe that the larger and more ostentatious of these imposing vessels were ever used for drinking. In both the different phases of the classical revival, in the late 18th and early 19th centuries, handleless goblets (q.v.) of convenient size were available in large numbers for those who wished to drink from silver cups. It is probably

Two-handled cup, c. 1806   *Two-handled cup, c. 1810*

significant that these should have appeared at a time when simple, functional two-handled cups of similar capacity had ceased to be fashionable.

Cut-card work: a method of decorating silver objects by cutting out shapes such as leaf-forms from sheet metal and soldering them to the surface. Cut-card work was first used to a modest extent quite early in the reign of Charles II (1660–1685), but became especially popular in the last decade of the century and the reign of Queen Anne (1702–1714), when it was much used by immigrant Huguenot silversmiths.

D

Date-letter: a letter of the alphabet struck on plate after the assay (q.v.) and normally current for one year. The letters and the cartouches in which they are contained are varied to lessen the danger of confusion between one cycle and another. The practice began in London as the result of a statute of 1477 which, in addition to other provisions, made the entire body of London goldsmiths responsible for any dereliction of duty on the part of the Warden, whose task it was to strike the official marks on plate. Thereupon the goldsmiths, who knew the identity of the Warden for any particular year and wished to be able to obtain indemnity from him if necessary, introduced the date-letter by a private regulation, the first evidently being the Lombardic letter A for 1478.

Decanter-stand: *see* Bottle-stand.

Dessert spoon: *see* Spoon, dessert.

Dish: dishes of many kinds were made of silver from early times, but the variety increased in the second half of the 18th century and included dishes for meat, venison, vegetables, etc. One of the most sought-after is the entrée dish. *See* Dish, entrée.

Dish, chafing: a covered dish, often rectangular with rounded corners, placed over a source of heat such as a spirit lamp to keep food hot. Chafing dishes are chiefly of 19th-century origin.

Dish-cross: a device for protecting the table from hot dishes, replacing the obsolete dish-ring (q.v.) and introduced in about 1740. A dish-cross consisted of two rotating silver rings, one above the other, with two silver bars extending from opposite sides of each. These four bars had feet, and supports attached above, which could be slid along the bars to

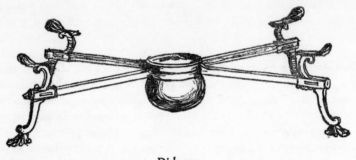

Dish-cross

accommodate dishes of varying size. There was frequently a small spirit lamp in the centre.

Dish, entrée: a covered silver dish, about 30 cm long, for the entrée, which usually signified, in England, the course between the fish and the joint. Entrée dishes were introduced in the second half of the 18th century and were mostly oblong with rounded corners, though they might be concave-sided with something of the appearance of cushions. The covers of the latter were often high in the centre and with permanent ring-handles, but the straight-sided variety, which was commoner after 1800, usually had a flat cover of about the same depth as the dish. The handle of this was often detachable, so that the cover could be used in an inverted position if required. A less frequent type had a compartment for hot water to maintain the heat of the contents. Most entrée dishes were plain except round the borders, which might have small gadroons or fine reeds.

Dish-ring: a silver ring for supporting a hot bowl or dish and raising it above the surface of the table. A reference in 1697 to 'Rings for a Table', in an inventory of plate, seems to suggest that dish-rings were already in existence in England before the end of the 17th century, but the earliest surviving examples date from the beginning of the 18th century and are exceedingly rare. They were generally superseded by the dish-cross (q.v.) in about 1740 and it is probable that, once they had been banished from the dining-room, most of them were melted down. Mention should be made, however, of an example of 1774 preserved in the Birmingham Assay Office. It has a wooden side handle of baluster-shape and a heater in the centre, but by this time, such objects were generally quite obsolete in England. In Ireland, however, their incidence increased from the middle of the 18th century onwards. Early specimens were fairly low, some being less than 8 cm high. All were spool-shaped, that is, the sides were concave and widened towards the rim and the base. These were chased and pierced with various kinds of ornament which often included rococo scrolls mingled sometimes with rather naïve bucolic scenes. The piercing was functional as well as decorative, for it lessened the conduction of heat. This ornament

Dish-ring, c. 1760

continued throughout the 18th century and beyond, despite the introduction of neo-classical elements in the last quarter of the century. From about 1760, the height was generally increased to 10 cm or more. The Adam style usually manifested itself in regular and somewhat mechanical piercing, sometimes with applied swags, medallions etc., but these are far less pleasing than earlier specimens. The incorrect jargon name 'potato rings' is often applied to these objects in both England and Ireland. It is necessary to examine the hall marks of any example encountered, as numerous reproductions, especially in the rococo style, have been produced even in the 20th century.

Dish, sweetmeat: a small silver dish, sometimes partly pierced, and without a handle, intended for such Georgian sweetmeats as orange chips.

85

Douter: an alternative to the extinguisher (q.v.) for putting out a candle, consisting of a scissor-like object terminating in flat plates between which the wick was pressed. Douters appeared in the 1690s, but never became as popular as the more convenient extinguishers and are consequently very rare.

Drawback mark: a mark on plate indicating drawback or refund of duty already paid, applied to silver objects which were exported. The mark consisted of a figure of Britannia incuse (hollow), contained in an irregular cartouche of modified rectangular shape with the right-hand side curving inward at the top. The mark was current from 1 December 1784 to 24 July 1785 and is rare in England for obvious reasons.

Draw plate: a steel plate pierced with holes of various shapes and sizes for reducing silver wire, which was mostly used for edge-mouldings.

Dredger: a fairly modern name for a large caster (q.v.).

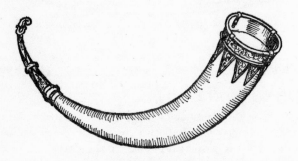

Anglo-Saxon drinking horn

Drinking horn: part of an ox-horn, tapering to a point, often mounted in silver and forming an arc-shaped drinking vessel. There are surviving examples and mounts from the Anglo-Saxon period, and so many were illustrated in contemporary illuminated manuscripts that it is evident that they must have existed in large numbers. Some had only silver lip-bands, many were tipped with a decorative finial at the pointed end as well. Their popularity declined after the Norman conquest, but occasional examples were made as late as the 15th century. From the 14th century, drinking horns were usually provided with two legs so that they could be stood on a flat surface instead of having to be retained in the hand until they were empty. Many were of very large capacity.

Dublin

Dublin: Irish goldsmiths were producing work of superb quality as early as the 10th century, but although there were documentary references to silversmithing activities in Dublin during the middle ages, no regular system of marking seems to have been in operation before 1605. In that year, the City Council published a resolution which included the provisions that every silversmith should use a personal mark and that the appropriate officials should have a stamp with a lion, a harp and a castle. Not one example of plate bearing these marks has survived, although they were current until 1637, when the Dublin goldsmiths petitioned King Charles I praying to be incorporated by royal charter. The charter was granted the same year, the marks prescribed in it being a crowned harp and the maker's mark. An annual date-letter began to be used in addition from 1638 by a regulation of the guild, but all three marks were made obligatory by a statute of 1729. Despite this, however, date-letters were frequently omitted, especially after about 1760, so that one is often able to date objects only on stylistic grounds and by reference to the identity of the maker. The payment of duty on wrought plate, which was imposed to raise funds for the improvement of agriculture, was evidenced from 1731 by a mark with a figure of Hibernia. Care should be taken not to confuse this with the English Britannia mark, though the Act of 1696 was never extended to Ireland. The mark of the sovereign's head, which had been compulsory on English plate since 1 December 1784, was not applied to Irish silver until 1807, and continued to be used, as in England, until 1890.

87

Dundee: records of Dundee silversmiths begin in the mid-16th century and surviving examples of plate from the early 17th century show that the town mark was a two-handled pot of flowers. Sometimes, from the late 18th century, the name of the town was used instead. There are no records of Dundee plate made after 1840.

Duty mark: a mark, indicating the payment of duty on British plate, in the form of the heads of successive sovereigns from 1 December 1784 to 30 April 1890, i.e.: George III, George IV, William IV and Victoria. The marks of the first three continued to be applied for a few years after the sovereign's death.

E

Ecuelle: a French porringer with two flat, horizontal handles and a cover. Some were very wide, though the bowls were invariably shallow as in the case of English porringers. A few were made in England in the early 18th century, chiefly by immigrant Huguenots.

Edinburgh, 1681

Edinburgh: it is not known precisely when silver artefacts began to be made in Scotland, as many early pieces were of native or Irish gold rather than silver; but evidence begins to accumulate from the late 7th century onwards. Surviving Pictish silver objects consist mostly of massive ceremonial chains for personal adornment, but from the beginning of the 8th century, greater variety occurred and many exotic influences including Irish, Scandinavian and German affected the design and ornament of, for example, reliquaries, secular brooches and armlets. Gilding and niello (q.v.) were well understood as in England and Ireland. There is a disastrous gap in evidence concerning part of the middle ages owing to the looting of Scottish plate by the English in the 12th century. Again, in the late 13th century, a wide range of plate, both liturgical and secular, found its way into London melting-pots, while the Reformation in the 16th century accounted for the destruction of much old and contemporary silver that remained in Edinburgh and elsewhere. In the capital city, chief centre of the craft, regulations governing its surveillance appeared in the second half of the 15th century and contained provisions whose purpose, like those of England, was to protect the buying public against fraud. At this time, the gold-smiths belonged to an incorporation of 'Hammermen', other members of which included armourers and makers of sword-hilts, but by 1525, they were an independent body. Since 1457, it had been obligatory for the mark of the 'dene' (deacon, warden, or assay-master) to be struck on plate as evidence of quality, together with that of the maker, and al-though the identity of the latter, which provides rough indications of date, is ascertainable from records kept from 1525, and the town mark of a castle was used from 1485, date-letters did not begin until 1681. From 1759, when Hugh Gordon was assay-master, a thistle was substituted for his initials as a guarantee of standard, and has been applied ever since in addition to the town mark (a castle) and the maker's mark. In 1784, the sovereign's head mark was introduced and continued up to 1890. *See* Duty mark.

Egg and dart

Egg and dart: otherwise known as Egg and tongue: a type of repeat-ing border ornament of classical origin used on plate from the renais-sance onwards and consisting of rows of ovolos with arrow-heads between them.

Egg-frame: a silver frame containing egg-cups, introduced in the late 18th century, sometimes having a central receptacle for salt and accompanied by its own spoons, the whole being of silver.

Electro-plating: the process of coating base metal with silver by electrolysis. A patent was taken out by Wright of Birmingham in 1840 in association with G. H. and H. Elkington, and the process rapidly superseded other methods. Electro-plating has sometimes been used to conceal discoloration caused by alterations to antique silver.

Electrum: an alloy of gold and silver used in classical times but very seldom afterwards.

Embossing: producing raised ornament on the outer surface of an object from the inside, by means of the hammer, snarling iron (q.v.) or punches. There is a modern tendency to draw a distinction between this and the process designated by the French term *repoussé* work, on the ground that the latter implies, not only embossing, but also chasing. But the distinction is invalid since, in practice, embossed motifs were always chased round the edges to give them definition.

Engraving: decorating the surface of silver with linear designs by means of a graver or burin, which cut thin furrows in the metal. This was the normal method for delineating coats of arms, crests and monograms.

Entrée dish: *see* Dish, entrée.

Epergne: a word which does not exist in the French language, but which may have been formed in England from *épargne* – an economy or saving. *See* Centrepiece.

Étui, c. 1780

Étui: a small flattened cylindrical case with a hinged cover, for needles, tooth-picks etc., common in silver and other materials in the late 18th century.

Ewer, c. 1580

Ewer: a jug used in association with a basin (q.v.) in which diners washed their hands before and after meals. Silver ewers often figured in medieval wills and inventories, but none has survived from before the 16th century, when their form and ornament were under renaissance influence. After the general adoption of forks for eating in the second half of the 17th century, ewers declined in incidence and eventually ceased to have any practical purpose.

Exeter, 1701

Exeter: there is evidence of the presence of goldsmiths in Exeter as early as the 14th century, but no distinctive town mark seems to have been used until the second half of the 16th century, when it took the form of a letter X, varying in detail. What appear to have been date-letters began to occur sporadically at the same time, but no regular system was in operation until 1701. The Act of 1696 which imposed the Britannia standard (q.v.) was not extended to Exeter specifically until 1700, with effect from the following year, and the town mark then became a distinctive triple-towered castle. After the higher standard ceased to be compulsory, the lion passant was used to indicate Sterling as it had on rare occasions previously, but a lion's or leopard's head, similar to the London mark, occurred as well as the castle until 1778. The Exeter assay office was closed in 1883.

F

Feeding-cup: *see* Spout cup.

Fender: silver fenders, known at the time as 'hearth rods', occurred in wealthy households in the reign of Charles II (1660–1685), but none is known to have survived.

Fiddle pattern: *see* Spoons.

Fire-dogs: *see* Andirons.

Fire-gilding: *see* Mercury gilding.

Fish-servers: a garniture comprising a fish-slice (q.v.) or large silver knife and a broad-headed fork; mostly 19th century.

Fish-slice, c. 1810

Fish-slice: a trowel-like object used to serve fish. It first appeared in England in the second quarter of the 18th century, but most existing examples are later. The forms of the pierced blades and the handles varied. Some blades were shaped like broad leaves, others were like builders' trowels, while those of the early 19th century were asymmetrical, having a single edge and an indentation at the back near the point. Handles in the 18th century might have a rounded end like that of a contemporary spoon or fork, or blade and handle were made separately, the second being somewhat like that of a knife, hollow and filled with a resin compound. In the early 19th century, most handles were in one piece with the rest and of the fiddle pattern.

Flagon: a name which began to be applied in the early 17th century to a kind of tall tankard of large capacity, previously known as a livery pot (q.v.), which was used either for drinking or for serving liquor into smaller vessels. Large silver flasks were also sometimes called flagons.

Flask: it is not known when silver flasks first began to be made and none has survived from before the middle years of the 16th century. They had flattened, bulbous bodies and chain handles. These early examples may have had a functional purpose though they were uncommon, but during the next phase in the late 17th and early 18th centuries, they were probably merely ostentatious. They are sometimes called pilgrim bottles, wine-bottles, or flagons.

Flatware: *see* Spoons and Forks.

Flutes, Fluting: decoration consisting of narrow hollows with straight or sometimes curved sides; introduced in the renaissance period in the first half of the 16th century when they often alternated with gadroons (q.v.). Fluting was especially prevalent on various kinds of plate made by immigrant Huguenots in the early 18th century and gained renewed vigour during the Adam (q.v.) period.

Font-shaped cup: a low standing cup, introduced in about 1500, having a short trumpet-shaped stem and a shallow bowl with straight sides. A specimen of 1503, belonging to the Worshipful Company of Goldsmiths of London, is equipped with a cover. *See* Cup, standing.

Fork: although it is evident that silver forks were known in England as early as the 9th century, and small 'sucket forks' were used in the later middle ages for sweetmeats, larger versions were not widely considered necessary at table until the last quarter of the 17th century. Even though they began to become fashionable when the Monarchy was restored in 1660, their general adoption was resisted for many years. Forks of the Charles-II period might have two, three, or four prongs, three being the most usual. Stems were identical with those of contemporary spoons and were of flattened rectangular section, broadening out into three lobes known as the trifid or trefid end. The same type persisted into the early 18th century, especially in Exeter, but in the 1690s another shape appeared. This was known as the wavy end and represented a modification of the trifid, with the lobes merging into each other; at the same time, stems became more rounded in section. Both the trifid and wavy ends had the central projection bent over so that it caused no discomfort in the palm of the hand. The wavy end remained prevalent for at least fifteen years after 1700, overlapping a new type which was introduced early in the century. This terminal, which was thickened and smoothly

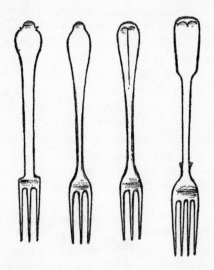

Forks, left to right: Trifid, c. 1680; Wavy end, c. 1700; Old English, c. 1715; Fiddle pattern, c. 1810

rounded, is called the Old English pattern and continued in use beyond the end of the 18th century. In the third quarter of the century, four prongs began to become more usual than three, though the latter, and occasionally two prongs, lingered on here and there until about 1800.

Early in the 19th century, the fiddle pattern was introduced from France, where it had been in use since about 1760. This had a broad end which narrowed suddenly inward to a parallel-sided stem with two small, projecting shoulders just above the prongs. This pattern, together with an elaborate derivative known as the King's pattern, which appeared during the Regency (q.v.), remained current throughout the 19th century and beyond. *See* also Spoons.

Freedom box: a silver casket in which the scroll, conferring the freedom of a city, was presented to the grantee.

Funnel: *see* Wine-funnel.

Furniture: there are references to items of silver furniture, or furniture covered with silver plates, in documents of the early 16th century, but survivals from any age are naturally of the utmost rarity, and the earliest period to yield any actual examples is that following the restoration of the Monarchy in 1660. It is evident from the diary of John Evelyn and other sources that large quantities existed in Whitehall Palace in the reign of Charles II, but most of this has vanished. A certain amount remains in the Royal Collection, which includes a pair of candle-stands of pillar-and-claw form and two tables, one of which is of wood covered with sheet silver. The other table, which was presented to William III by the City of London in the late 17th century, is almost entirely of silver, with only enough wood and iron in its construction to prevent the buckling of the soft precious metal. The legs are in the form of terminal female caryatids of great artistic merit. Silver furniture became outmoded in the early 18th century, but a plain table of the period made for the Earl of Oxford is owned by the Duke of Portland, while another, fashioned in 1742, is still preserved in Russia. More striking than these is the massive silver throne with eagle-head arms and cabriole legs with claw-and-ball feet, which was made in London for Peter the Great in 1713 and is to be seen in the Hermitage Museum, Leningrad.

G

Gadroons, Gadrooning: ornament consisting of convex lobes either straight or curved, often alternating with flutes (q.v.), occurring chiefly on the edges of silver objects from the early 16th century; also known as knurling or nulling.

Gilding: *see* Mercury gilding.

Glasgow: though Glasgow was a university town, in the 15th and 16th centuries it was a relatively unimportant burgh and, until about the middle of the 17th century, was of less prominence as a silversmithing centre than Aberdeen. The Hammermen of Glasgow, which later included such famous craftsmen as James Simpson the swordsmith, were incorporated in 1536, but although plate was undoubtedly made at a very early period, date-letters and a town mark did not begin to be used until 1681. The town mark was the arms of the burgh:an oak-tree with a fish and a bell, and continued to be applied until the assay office closed in 1964, but date-letters fell out of use in about 1710 and were not used again in a regular manner until 1819, when the mark of a lion rampant, which had first appeared as a sign of quality in 1811, became compulsory at the same time.

Goblet: another name for a standing cup, supported on a stem and foot.

Goldsmiths' Company: the Worshipful Company of Goldsmiths of London received its charter from King Edward III in 1327.

Gothic: ornament deriving from Gothic architecture was found in many branches of English craftsmanship from the early 13th century, when England began to evolve an indigenous style, but its incidence in relation to silver was greatest in the 14th, 15th and 16th centuries. It occurred on both secular and ecclesiastical plate, the chief techniques being cast work, engraving and chasing. An extremely popular device was a cast gallery consisting of a circuit of small, concave-sided cusps surmounted by flower-heads. These galleries were found round the feet of standing cups and salts and the lower edges of covers. Similar ornament occurred in contemporary woodwork and stone-carving. *See* Thurible.

Gravy-spoon: *see* Spoon, gravy.

Guilloche

Guilloche: running ornament of classical origin comprising counter-changed ogee curves producing rows of almost circular compartments; occurring in England from the introduction of the renaissance style in the early 16th century to the Regency (q.v.) period and applied by means of various techniques.

H

Hall-marking: in this section we are concerned only with London, certain other centres being dealt with under their respective headings, such as Dublin, Edinburgh, etc. Although a Royal ordinance of 1238 decreed that wrought plate should be of the same standard as the coinage, i.e.: Sterling (q.v.), it was not until 1300 that a compulsory mark was prescribed as evidence of quality. In that year an Act was passed which provided that the wardens of the London goldsmiths should assay all wrought plate and, if it was of the legal standard, stamp it with a leopard's head. This mark was taken from the Royal arms of England and it should be noted, in this connection, that the heraldic term 'leopard' denoted a lion passant. In 1363, an Act of Edward III ordered that every master goldsmith should have a personal mark which was to be struck on the piece after it had been assayed and stamped with the leopard's head – described in the statute as 'the King's Mark'. The object of this was clearly to enable any default to be brought home to the actual maker.

An Act of Edward IV in 1477 referred to the leopard's head as being 'crowned' and it may probably be presumed that this addition to the mark was introduced in the year of the statute. The same Act made the entire fraternity of London goldsmiths answerable for any dereliction of duty on the part of the warden, whereupon the goldsmiths themselves introduced another mark to enable them to obtain indemnity from the official responsible. This mark was the date-letter, to be changed annually, beginning with the Lombardic letter A for 1478, and as the identity of the warden for any particular year was known its use meant that responsibility could be fixed without difficulty.

In 1542, Henry VIII began to debase the coinage; by 1544 it consisted of only half silver and half alloy and the following year became even worse. This seems to have persuaded the goldsmiths to adopt some means of reassuring the buying public as to the quality of wrought plate, which remained unchanged. They accordingly introduced another mark consisting of a complete lion passant guardant which was crowned for the first six years, and although the coinage was restored to the Sterling standard by Queen Elizabeth in 1560, the lion passant continued to be used on plate to denote Sterling silver. As the leopard's head had had its original function usurped by the lion passant, it soon came to be recognized as the mark of the London assay office.

During the Civil War, huge quantities of plate were melted down for conversion into coin to pay the troops of King and Parliament, but after the restoration of the Monarchy, demand for domestic silver was so great that vast amounts of coin began to be melted for conversion into plate. By 1696 this practice had become a serious contributory factor to a grave financial crisis, and an Act was passed, with effect from the following year, compulsorily raising the standard of wrought plate to the Britannia standard (q.v.) to prevent the use of coin as a raw material by silversmiths. The Act remained in force until June 1720, and during this period, the higher standard was indicated by a figure of Britannia, the London mark was a lion's head erased, and the maker's mark comprised the first two letters of the surname.

Another mark began to be applied from 1 December 1784 to denote payment of duty (*see* Duty mark). This took the form of the sovereign's head beginning with that of George III. Until May 1786, a punch with a convex image was used, so that the mark was incuse (hollow), but thereafter it was in relief like all other marks.

In 1821, the leopard's head ceased to be crowned and at the same time the lion passant ceased to be guardant (regarding the observer) and simply looked straight ahead.

Hammers: the following hammers are among the silversmith's most important tools. Bossing hammer: for raising protuberances by striking the metal on the other side. Chasing hammer: for striking the top of a tracing tool so that it compresses the metal in a line and moves forward with each stroke. Planishing hammer: for levelling out smaller hammer marks prior to polishing. Raising hammer: for raising hollow-ware from flat sheet silver. *See* also Stakes.

Hanap (Anglo-Saxon hnaepp): a medieval term probably signifying a large standing cup with a cover. *See* Cup, standing.

Hash spoon: *see* Spoon, hash.

Honey-pot, c. 1800

Honey-pot: silver or silver-gilt honey-pots achieved sudden popularity in the late 18th century and continued after 1800 with little change. The silver parts consisted typically of a flat circular dish supporting a domed cover in the form of a skep, or beehive, the straw and bindings being represented in a more or less realistic manner. The famous London silversmith Paul Storr was a skilled exponent of the style from the last decade of the 18th century until well into the Regency period.

Horn: *see* Drinking horn.

Hull: there were probably goldsmiths in Kingston-upon-Hull in the late 13th century, but no records exist from prior to the early 15th century. Examples of plate are uncommon and generally consist of various kinds of drinking vessels and spoons. Activity apparently ceased altogether in the early 18th century and there is no evidence that express legal recognition was ever extended to any confraternity which may have existed. Nevertheless, there must have been some degree of organisation of the craft. Up to the end of the 16th century, a capital letter H was used as a town mark, but thereafter, three crowns, the arms of the town, were stamped on plate, occasionally with the letter H as well. Hull was one of the few centres where tankards of Scandinavian type were made in the 17th century.

I

Inkstand: a Victorian name for what was previously known as a standish (q.v.).

Inverness: the earliest known piece of Inverness plate is a quaich (q.v.) made in about 1640 and bearing the letters INS, an abbreviation of the name of the town. This remained the usual town mark until about 1880, after which no more plate seems to have been assayed. Inverness was of no great comparative importance as a silversmithing centre, but has been mentioned here because spoons are sometimes encountered.

J

Jug, cream or milk: it appears that milk or cream did not begin to be drunk with tea until about 1700; consequently, no silver jugs to contain them were made before the early 18th century and remained uncommon until habits underwent a general change. The first type had a

Cream-jug, c. 1720   Cream-jug, c. 1750

Swag-bellied cream-jug, c. 1750   Irish cream-jug, c. 1750

baluster-shaped body with a scroll handle and was mounted on a foot-ring. Jugs of a similar kind were more plentiful in the second quarter of the century, when several other types existed as well, and remained popular until about 1750. A rare variety of the reign of Queen Anne (1702–1714) was like a miniature ewer, supported on a stem and foot. In the 1730s, three short feet began to be used as an alternative to the foot-ring, some of the accompanying bodies being ovoid and of heavy, cast silver, others being baluster-shaped and wrought. The second variety was especially prevalent during the rococo (q.v.) period and was often decorated by embossing with appropriate ornament, though plain examples, which were cheaper, occurred as well. At the same time, a swag-bellied shape, used also on other hollowware, appeared as a rival to the baluster and was particularly common in the 1760s. It continued far into the Adam (q.v.) period, often embellished with obsolete rococo decoration. A number of outré types occurred in the second half of the century, some being too scarce to warrant discussion, but mention must be made of milk-jugs in the form of a cow, most of them being the work of John Schuppe, who was possibly of Dutch origin or extraction. The curled tail formed the handle and the milk was poured out through the cow's mouth. The jug was filled by an aperture in the creature's back which was closed by a shaped lid surmounted by a large and unattractive fly. This type, which was neither a good jug nor a good model of a cow, has increased in popularity among collectors for no very obvious reason. Meanwhile, Irish silversmiths had begun, in about 1750, to make use of a shape which had already occurred sparsely in England in the second quarter of the century. This was somewhat like an inverted helmet and widened slightly towards the rim.

Cream-jug, c. 1780

There was often a narrow applied moulding running round the body. The three feet, reminiscent of cabriole legs, frequently bore a lion's mask at the point where they were soldered to the body of the jug. Some were plain, others were embossed with low-relief rococo ornament. Very few had complete sets of hall marks. These handsome objects, which are regarded as typically Irish, continued to be made for upwards of twenty years. They were attractive, poured well and were easy to clean.

In the Adam period, the neo-classical style affected the shape of these jugs in Britain and Ireland and they were made to look as nearly as possible like urns, often with square feet. Embossing was seldom resorted to, decoration, when it occurred at all, usually consisting of applied medallions, fluting, bright-cut engraving, or bead-mouldings (q.q.v.). In about 1800, bodies became wider and more squat and rested most commonly on their own flat bases, though some had small ball-feet while others had short stems. The capacity of these was noticeably greater than that of previous types. By this time, homogeneous tea-sets

Cream-jug, c. 1810

were in fairly general use and their manufacture increased in the early 19th century. Like many contemporary tea-pots, jugs were often decorated with bold gadroons or reeds round the lower part of the body, some being provided with enclosed spouts instead of pouring-lips.

Jug, hot milk: a description sometimes applied to what is otherwise known as a hot-water jug or a shaving jug, the purpose of such objects being not always clear.

Jug, hot-water: a more general term for what is known alternatively as a hot-milk jug or sometimes a shaving jug. The vessels in question display a common feature in the wooden handle, or a silver handle bound with cane, which indicates that the contents were hot. They began to appear in the early 18th century and are sometimes to be seen in contemporary paintings. Their proportions were similar to those of a coffee-pot, but they were equipped with a pouring-lip rather than a distinct spout.

Jug, shaving: it is known that silver jugs accompanied shaving bowls in the early 16th century and they probably existed before this, but no examples have survived, so far as the author is aware, from before the early 18th century. Queen-Anne shaving jugs might have insulated handles and flattened baluster-shaped bodies with a pouring-lip, but they were not always of this form and the handle was sometimes of silver, so that it would have been necessary to hold it with a cloth when the jug was full of hot water. Contemporary representations of tea-drinking scenes often show jugs of a similar kind, so it is not always possible to be dogmatic about the purpose of all specimens encountered. It is possible, of course, that they were used in several ways. The period of their greatest popularity was apparently the first half of the 18th century, after which they tended to be superseded by jugs made of china.

K

Kantharos: *see* Cup, two-handled.

Kent, William (1684–1748): like Robert Adam (q.v.) later, William Kent considered it the duty of an architect to design, not only buildings, but also their more important contents in order to establish a general harmony. This was a novel conception at the time. With the Earl of Burlington, he was a pioneer of the Palladian revival in England, and his ideas dominated design until shortly before the middle of the 18th century. In 1744, John Vardy published some of the designs of the architect Inigo Jones, creator of the early 17th-century Banqueting House in Whitehall, London, and William Kent, including fourteen pages of Kent's designs for domestic plate. They were in the grand manner and in a somewhat heavy neo-classical style. Some of them were not executed until the Regency period, when they accorded with the contemporary taste for massiveness; but some of them included ornament of a character which was a prophetic foretaste of the Adam style. His designs for plate, however, had little effect during his lifetime owing to the popularity of the rococo style which was gaining strength at the time his designs were published.

Kettle: silver kettles do not appear to have formed part of the tea equipage until after the death of Charles II (1685) and although a rare example made in 1694 still survives, none earlier than the Queen-Anne period is likely to be met with. The normal type of this period echoed the shape of the contemporary pyriform tea-pot (q.v.), but was provided with a swing-handle insulated at the centre. Like later variants, it was supported on a silver stand with a lamp for heating the water. In the 1720s, an alternative spherical form was introduced and continued up to about 1750, long after the pear-shape had fallen into disuse. In the middle of the century a swag-bellied or inverted pear-shape was used for kettles as for many other objects and persisted until about 1765. A few kettles of various types were made in the late 18th and early 19th centuries, but they had begun to fall out of fashion in about 1760 in favour of the urn (q.v.).

King's head mark: *see* Duty mark.

Kitchen pepper: a modern name for a cylindrical pepper caster with a rounded cover and a single scrolled handle.

Knop: a protuberance in the stem of a standing cup etc.

Knurling or nulling: an alternative name for gadroons (q.v.).

'Kitchen pepper', c. 1720

L

Label: *see* Bottle ticket.

Punch ladle, c. 1750

Ladle: ladles can be divided into two main categories – those concerned with liquor and those concerned with food.

Punch-ladle: the earliest documentary reference to punch (*see* Bowl, punch) known to the author is of the year 1632, but one hears nothing of ladles for serving it until considerably later. It is unlikely that silver punch ladles were made in the reign of Charles II when silver punch-bowls first appeared, and even in the early 18th century the liquor was sometimes poured from china jugs. Furthermore, the English composer, Henry Purcell (1659–1695) wrote a round which included the words 'Dip your dish fair around to all jolly punch-drinkers', and as he was well acquainted with drinking matters, it may be presumed that he would not have used the term 'dish' if a ladle had been the normal means of serving punch.

Probably, the first punch-ladles were made towards the end of the 17th century, the original type continuing after 1700. They had large circular bowls and tubular silver stems ending in a dome finial. Bowl and stem were at a slight angle. Certain large spoons of the same period, with similar stems and capacious oval bowls, are sometimes described as punch ladles, but this is probably erroneous, as bowl and stem were more or less in a straight line and such a utensil would have been inconvenient for dipping into a deep punch-bowl. It is impossible to determine precisely when the conventional punch ladle first came on the scene, partly because punch was often served cold, so that a stem of wood or whalebone, almost universal later, would not have been necessary to protect the hand from conducted heat, but they began to be fairly plentiful in the second quarter of the 18th century. There were considerable variations in shape of no chronological significance, so that bowls might be circular, oval, single-lipped, double-lipped, or in the form of shells. After 1740, many were hammered from captured Spanish crown-pieces so that the original inscription round the edge of the coin encircled the rim of the ladle. Many of all periods had a coin, either of gold or silver, set in the base. Punch ladles of the late 18th century tended to be flimsier than earlier examples.

Toddy-ladle: a smaller version of the punch ladle in the late 18th and early 19th centuries. Its appearance coincided with the introduction of toddy, a powerful spirituous compound, and it was used as an alternative to a bulbous glass pipette called a toddy-lifter.

Sauce-ladle: in the form of a miniature soup ladle and evolving in much the same manner, the sauce ladle began to be used from just after the middle of the 18th century in association with the sauce tureen (q.v.).

Soup-ladle: lack of evidence makes it unprofitable to speculate about soup ladles of the first half of the 18th century, although they undoubtedly existed at the time. The ends of the silver handles were the same as those of spoons (q.v.), that is, Old English followed by the fiddle pattern in the early 19th century, with an occasional Onslow-pattern end just after the middle of the 18th century. Bowls might be circular or, less frequently, in the form of scallop shells, but the fiddle pattern type was usually accompanied by an oval bowl with the handle attached to one of the longer sides. The same considerations applied to sauce-ladles.

Lemon-strainer: while orange-strainers were in use as early as the beginning of the 16th century, lemon-strainers do not seem to have existed before silver punch-bowls in the late 17th century. They varied somewhat in size but very little in style, and always consisted of a shallow circular bowl pierced in various ways and with two flat handles, one on each side. The handles might be solid, in openwork, or made of wire.

Lincoln: although there was a mint at Lincoln in the 9th century and this usually implied silversmithing activity as well, there is, unfortunately, no firm evidence that plate was made there apart from a few post-Reformation communion cups in the 16th century. It is mentioned here simply to remind students that Sir Charles Jackson was mistaken in ascribing the mark of a fleur-de-lis to Lincoln.

Livery pot, c. 1570

Livery pot (French *livrer*, to deliver): a pot, with one or more handles, from which liquor was served into drinking vessels. They are often to be seen in medieval manuscript illustrations standing on domestic cup boards, but silver examples have not survived from before the 16th century. Those of the Elizabethan period (1558–1603) mostly had bodies in the form of strongly-emphasised architectural balusters, though it seems likely that the shape derived immediately from that of a common type of pottery vessel rather than from architecture. The pot was surmounted by a low, hinged lid attached to the top of the handle, which was hollow and of scroll-form. It was provided with a thumb-piece and in all these respects was similar, apart from its large size, to the earliest known type of English silver tankard (q.v.). It was supported, however, in a different manner, being mounted on a stem and foot like those of a standing cup. This kind of livery pot was almost certainly employed only for serving, but another variant, of cylindrical form, was used alternatively for drinking beer and may therefore be considered as a large tankard as well as a livery pot. During the first quarter of the 17th century, when plate was becoming simpler and was usually left ungilded, these pots began to be called 'flagons' and the term 'livery pot' gradually fell out of use.

Lloyd's patriotic fund: a fund established by Lloyd's of London after the Battle of Trafalgar (1805) to finance, in the first instance, presentations to senior naval officers who had taken part in the battle. In particular, these took the form of lavish silver-gilt two-handled cups or vases varying in size but of similar design, based on classical Greek originals and interpreted by John Flaxman. A general distinguishing feature was the vertical handles curling inward or outward to form volutes and looking somewhat like the shoot of a fern. *See* Cup, two-handled.

London: nothing is known about the organisation of the London goldsmiths until 1180, when a fine was imposed upon them by King Henry II for forming a guild without a licence from the Crown. They probably never paid the fine owing to their importance in the country's financial system, and it may be presumed that some form of association was maintained among them. They were granted a charter by King Edward III in 1327 and the prestige and authority of the Worshipful Company of Goldsmiths has endured over the centuries. They still have considerable legal powers, which are chiefly exercised to maintain the honour and integrity of the craft. The mark of the London Assay

London, 1544

Office, which has always been the most important in England, was a lion's head on Sterling silver. It was crowned until 1821. *See* Britannia standard.

Loving cup: a general term for a cup of any kind which was used by two or more persons who pledged each other from the same vessel in turn. An example is afforded by many two-handled cups of the 18th century, though there is little doubt that the primary purpose of the larger specimens was decorative.

M

Magdalen cup: *see* Beaker.

Marrow-scoop, c. 1720

Marrow-scoop: an implement with a trough-shaped end or ends, for extracting marrow from bones. A late 17th-century example has been noted with the scoop in the handle of a long three-pronged fork, but most specimens of the 18th and early 19th centuries were either double-ended, for bones of different sizes or, more rarely, were combined with table spoons.

Mazarine: a large perforated silver dish, fitting over a shallow receptacle for hot water, first intended for savoury meat dishes such as *ragoûts* and later for fish. The name derives either from Cardinal Mazarin or his niece Hortense de Mancini, and it was almost certainly introduced to London society in the reign of Charles II by the exiled Chevalier de St Evremond, who also popularised sparkling champagne in England.

Mazer, c. 1380

Mazer: a wooden drinking bowl usually made of spotted maple, the name being cognate with an old German word meaning a spot. Mazers were often mounted in silver or silver-gilt and examples have survived from the 14th century, probably because too little precious metal was involved in their manufacture to warrant their destruction. The mounts generally comprised a band round the lip, known at the time as a 'cup band', and a boss in the centre of the internal base which was also called a 'print'. This was mostly decorated with translucent enamel or by engraving, with a coat of arms, a pictorial device, or a simple motif such as the sacred monogram IHS (*Jesus Hominum Salvator*). In the 15th century, the cup band tended to become deeper. As the fortunes of the owner of a mazer improved, he would sometimes have it mounted on a silver stem and foot in the prevailing style, thus converting it into a standing mazer, and the wooden bowl was occasionally replaced later by a silver one. Mazers persisted into the 16th century, Elizabethan examples usually having deep bowls and three or four vertical silver straps linking the cup band with the base.

Medallion: an oval or circular compartment containing a decorative device such as a head, figures of goddesses etc.; of classical origin and much used in the late 18th century. *See* Adam.

Medical silver: among other materials, silver was used for various items devoted to medical purposes, a rare 16th-century instrument-case in the possession of the Barber-Surgeons' Company of London being particularly fine. Some objects had domestic applications as well. These included porringers (q.v.) which sometimes served as bleeding bowls during a long period when cupping was regarded almost as a panacea, even as late as the 19th century. It is recorded that a man who was dying from loss of blood at the battle of Waterloo in 1815 was bled by a surgeon to improve his condition, and there were doubtless many other instances of unquestioning faith in this form of therapy.

In the Georgian period, physicians often carried in their pockets flattened silver cases rather like étuis (q.v.) containing from three to six small lancets, so that they could bleed patients whenever required. Complete cupping sets were also made and were contained in special cases. In addition to the receptacle for the extracted blood, which was sometimes made of glass like those used by some Greek physicians at the present day, they comprised a silver spirit lamp for heating the cup to create a vacuum in it, and a silver scarificator. This was a box-shaped instrument, which had been known in various forms since the 17th century, fitted with a spring-loaded battery of six to twelve small, curved blades. The box was held against the selected area of the body, and pressure on a trigger released the spring so that the blades went about 3 mm into the flesh. The heated cup was then applied and, as it cooled, the requisite quantity of blood was drawn out of the incisions.

Silver pap-boats (q.v.) were employed by physicians for administering various liquid or semi-liquid substances of a nutritive or therapeutic nature to debilitated patients. These utensils, however, were also used in domestic surroundings for feeding infants and invalids, but other silver objects were of an exclusively medical character. These included cylindrical instrument-cases fitted with such things as scissors, flexible probes, spatulae, dressing forceps and, in one example of the late 18th century, a female catheter. The last instrument was commonly of steel, but a spiral silver catheter about 35 cm long is preserved at the Royal College of Surgeons.

Another instrument for extracting fluid of a different kind was the trocar. A Roman example of bronze was found at Pompeii, but some were evidently made of silver in 18th-century England. A definition of 1706 described the instrument as 'a cane or pipe made of silver or steel, with a sharp pointed end used in tapping those who are troubled with dropsy'. One would like to think that the trocar troubled them less.

The existence of a silver nipple-shield, designed to obviate the further irritation of a part which had been made sore by the excessive enthusiasm of an infant, suggests that other quasi-medical items may have been fashioned from silver as well. The picture is doubtless falsified in some degree by the fact that if such things became obsolete, their intrinsic value probably caused them to be consigned to the melting-pot. One remarkable object, however, has fortunately survived the march of medical progress. This is an early substitute for plastic surgery, dating from the 19th century, consisting of a silver false nose mounted on a spectacle-frame of the same metal. The account of the way in which it came into the possession of the gentleman from whom it passed to the Royal College of Surgeons throws an interesting sidelight on differing tastes in the marital relationship. It clearly belonged to a lady whose natural charm was greater than her physical defects. 'The patient presented herself wearing the said apparatus. She was also deficient in teeth, as well as in palate, the result of large doses of mercury for the cure of syphilis. She was married. Some years later she returned, with the nose in her hand, saying that she had lost her husband and, marrying again, her present husband liked her better without the nose than with it. The nose was purchased for three pounds.'

Mercury-gilding, or fire-gilding: an ancient and efficient method of coating silver and other metals with a layer of gold; known to the ancient Greeks and of uncertain origin. Pure gold was melted in a crucible with mercury and the resultant amalgam was then painted over the surface of the object to be gilded. This was put on an iron plate over a fire. The heat drove off the mercury in a highly poisonous vapour, leaving the gold intimately associated with the silver, with some mingling of particles below the surface. Mercury-gilding was the standard method until the introduction of the inferior, but safer, electro-gilding in the 19th century.

Milk-jug: *see* Jug, cream or milk.

Mirror: apart from the small mirrors with silver frames which formed part of ladies' toilet sets (q.v.) in the 16th and 17th centuries, large looking-glasses were sometimes mounted in a similar manner, though examples are understandably rare. It will suffice to mention three in the Royal Collection. Two were presented by the City of London to Charles II and William III respectively. Both are over 2 metres high. The first is ornamented with flowers and amorini with two letters C on the cresting. The second has a frame decorated with fruit in relief and with the Royal arms on the cresting. The other, which is a great deal smaller and was described as having been made for the 'Queen Dowager', which might have been either Henrietta Maria or Catherine of Braganza, is less lavishly ornamented with acanthus foliage and bay leaves.

Monteith, c. 1690

Monteith: a bowl, about 30 cm in diameter, in which wine-glasses were cooled by suspending them by the feet through indentations in the rim, so that their bowls were immersed in cold water. The diarist

Anthony à Wood, writing in *Life and Times*, stated that monteiths were introduced in 1683 and were named after a Scotsman who affected notches round the hem of his cloak or coat. In the last decade of the 17th century, a dual-purpose vessel was devised with a detachable monteith rim. When this was removed, the bowl could be used for brewing punch. Monteiths fell out of favour in about 1720. *See* Bowl, punch.

Mote-skimmer

Mote-skimmer or strainer spoon: the size of a long tea-spoon, with a pierced bowl and a stem terminating in a spike. It was connected with the serving of tea and was almost certainly used to remove leaves from the surface of the beverage in the cup and to free the perforations at the base of the spout of the tea-pot from the inside. Early examples of the late 17th century had bowls pierced with simple holes, but later piercing was far more decorative. These spoons remained fashionable until the late 18th century.

Muffineer: a modern jargon name for a small caster (q.v.).

Mug: *see* Can or Mug.

Mustard-pot: dry mustard was used in England at least as early as the 16th century, sometimes mixed with sugar, but the earliest known reference to a silver mustard-pot relates to Prince Rupert's in 1670. Others evidently existed in some numbers before 1700, but surviving examples from before the middle of the 18th century are rare. Some were cylindrical or barrel-shaped, with a domed lid with or without a finial and a thumbpiece, and seem to have been called 'mustard tankards'. Others were oval, octagonal or hexagonal, occasionally mounted on feet but mostly resting on their own flat bases. Their production

Mustard-pot, c. 1785

increased enormously in the last quarter of the 18th century. The sides
of many were decoratively pierced in the contemporary fashion and
were fitted with blue glass liners whose production was by no means
confined to Bristol. The bottoms of such silver pots were seldom solid,
the base of the liner resting on a silver flange round the edge. Examples
of the early 19th century were often heavier than previously and many
were supported on feet. From the late 18th century, silver-mounted
mustard-pots of cut glass were often accommodated in cruet-frames.

Mustard spoon: special small spoons for mustard were known in the
late 17th century, but most surviving examples date from the second
half of the 18th century and are shaped like miniature ladles. It is
possible that salt-spoons were also used for mustard. In the early 19th
century, some mustard spoons had elongated bowls, broadening
towards the end.

N

Nautilus shell: in the 16th century, when English plate was under
fairly strong Germanic influence, the fashion of making drinking cups

out of silver-mounted nautilus shells was introduced from the Habsburg empire. The shell was carefully stripped down to the underlying mother-of-pearl and was then capped and rimmed with silver or silver-gilt and mounted on a silver stem and foot in the prevailing taste. Nautilus-shell cups never achieved any great popularity in England, owing partly, no doubt, to their bizarre appearance and fragility. Furthermore, one can never be quite certain of their origin. They might have been made by an English silversmith with a partiality for German designs, or a German silversmith resident in England, or they might have been imported from Nürnberg or Augsburg and stamped with the mark of the English silversmith who submitted them for assay at Goldsmiths' Hall.

Nef: a rare piece of domestic plate, occurring occasionally in royal and noble households in the middle ages and the renaissance, consisting of a silver model of a ship containing various table requisites.

Neo-classical style: *see* Adam.

Newcastle, 1702

Newcastle: there were evidently goldsmiths working in Newcastle upon Tyne as early as the 13th century, but nothing is known of their organisation until 1536, when they were incorporated in a guild which included other craftsmen. The fortunes of this guild fluctuated considerably and at times it contained no goldsmiths at all. However, although there seems to have been no regular assay office until after 1700, Newcastle plate stamped with a single-towered castle has survived from the middle of the 17th century. About twenty years later, three castles in a variable shield, arranged two and one as in the town arms, were used instead and continued as the Newcastle mark until the assay office closed in 1884. Its legal existence had commenced in 1702 and date-letters began to be used in the same year.

Niello (Latin, *nigellum*): an amalgam of silver, copper, lead and sulphur which, when fused into shaped recesses in the surface of silver artefacts, made decorative patterns in a lustrous black enamel. The technique was practised with great skill by Anglo-Saxon and Celtic goldsmiths before the Norman conquest and was particularly effective when juxtaposed with silver-gilt as, for example, on the mounts of drinking horns (q.v.), but it seems to have largely fallen out of favour by the beginning of the 15th century. Praiseworthy but unsuccessful attempts have been made to revive its popularity in modern times. Niello was much used in 19th-century Russia for the embellishment of snuff-boxes and the silver hilts and scabbard-furniture of sabres and daggers.

Norwich: there is documentary proof of the existence of goldsmiths in Norwich from the late 13th century, but although the city was authorised by an Act of Henry VI in 1423 to have its own mark, advantage of this was not taken until 1565. Regular assaying began in that year, the town mark being the city arms, a castle with a lion beneath; at the same time, makers' marks and date-letters began to be used as well. Thereafter, however, marking became varied and erratic, and no plate is known to have been assayed in the city after 1701.

Nutmeg-grater: a somewhat rare item of 18th-century silver, consisting of a small ovoid container. One end held the nutmeg while the other embodied a rasp for grating it.

O

Oil and vinegar frame: a small silver frame of the late 18th and early 19th centuries containing silver-mounted cut-glass bottles for oil and vinegar. *See* Cruet-frame.

Old English pattern: *see* Spoons.

Onslow pattern, c. 1750

Onslow pattern: an uncommon spoon-terminal found for about twenty years from the middle of the 18th century. It broadened out into a ribbed end which curved downward; named after Arthur Onslow, Speaker of the House of Commons. Forks with the same terminal are rarely encountered.

Ostrich-egg cup: standing cups made of ostrich eggs mounted in silver or silver-gilt were known in the medieval period, when they were ascribed to a fabulous monster, but none has endured from before the 16th century. Apart from the substance of the bowls, they were entirely similar to coco-nut cups (q.v.).

P

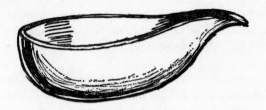

Pap-boat, c. 1750

Pap-boat: a shallow 18th-century silver vessel designed for administering semi-liquid food to infants or invalids. It was oval in shape with a pouring-lip at the narrower end and had neither a handle nor feet. Some have been converted later into cream-boats by the addition of these elements.

Parcel-gilt: partly gilt.

Paten: a miniature dish, usually in silver-gilt, used for administering the sacred wafer to communicants in church. When not in use, it usually stood on the top of the chalice as a cover. In the Elizabethan period, it often took the form of an actual cover with a small flattened finial.

Patera, plural paterae: a flat ornamental motif of classical architectural origin, either circular or oval, deriving from a shallow cup of the same name used for pouring libations in religious ceremonies. *See* Adam.

Peg tankard or pin tankard: this was defined as follows in the 18th-century *A Classical Dictionary of the Vulgar Tongue*: 'In or to a merry pin; almost drunk: an allusion to a sort of tankard, formerly used in the north, having silver pegs or pins set at equal distances from the top to the bottom; by the rules of good fellowship, every person drinking out of one of these tankards, was to swallow the quantity contained between two pins; if he drank more or less, he was to continue drinking till he ended at a pin; by this means persons unaccustomed to measure their draughts were obliged to drink the whole tankard. Hence, when a person was a little elevated with liquor, he was said to have drunk to a merry pin.'

Pins or pegs first occurred in tankards of Scandinavian inspiration made in Edinburgh, York, Hull and Newcastle from the late 1650s, but were also found later in more orthodox types in other centres including London. Their popularity did not extend beyond the first quarter of the 18th century.

Perfume-burner: silver perfume-burners are mentioned in inventories of the early 16th century and may well have existed before, but it is evident that they were never anything but uncommon and were confined to very wealthy households. They last occurred to any extent in the reign of Charles II, when silver domestic appointments attained an unprecedented lavishness. At this period they began to be called cassolets (French, *cassolettes*). The piercing of the covers was often extremely attractive.

Perth: the silversmiths of Perth were members of the Incorporation of Hammermen, but records of their activities date only from the early 16th century and give little information until after 1670. The earliest mark was a lamb with the banner of St Andrew, but this was replaced in the early 18th century by a double-headed eagle displayed. In the 19th century, the eagle sometimes had only one head. Manufacture appears to have ceased in about 1850 and nearly all plate bearing the Perth marks consists of flatware.

Pilgrim bottle: *see* Flask.

Plate: (*a*) a synonym for silver (cf. Spanish *plata*). In modern times, an unfortunate practice has developed of using the term incorrectly for what should be properly described as 'plated ware'. (*b*) Silver food-plates were widely used in the medieval period and some have survived from the 16th century. They displayed few evolutionary changes and were seldom of any great artistic interest with the exception of fruit-plates such as strawberry-dishes, which were often attractively decorated.

Plateau: a long, low platform with rounded ends, mostly supported on many small feet, running down the centre of a dining-table in the late 18th and early 19th centuries. Plateaux were often made in sections so that the length could be varied as required. They were made of various materials including silver.

Pomander (French, *pomme d'ambre*): a pierced silver container enclosing a perfumed ball or sponge, carried to mask unpleasant odours and as a guard against infection. It is evident, from the derivation of the name, that early examples contained a ball scented with ambergris. Some were carried in the hand, others were suspended round the neck by a silver chain. Pomanders were known in the medieval period but most extant examples, which are very scarce, are of 16th-century origin. The latter usually opened outward in sections, each with its own perfume. A few were in the form of human skulls. The pomander may be regarded as the ancestor of the later vinaigrette (q.v.).

Porringer, c. 1680

Porringer: a shallow vessel of variable width; with curved sides and one or two handles, to contain pottage, the word 'porridge' being a variant of this term. Pottage might consist of various semi-liquid foods including stew, thick vegetable soup, or a concoction of oatmeal, and it is interesting to note that a village with the homely name of Pease Pottage still exists in Sussex. Porringers were known in the medieval period, and in the Ordinances of the Pewterers of 1348, reference was made to them under the name *esquelles* (modern French, *écuelles*). It is possible that some were made of silver at the same time. They were doubtless familiar enough by the end of the 16th century, and in Shakespeare's play, *The Taming of the Shrew*, Petruchio complains to his haberdasher: 'This cap was moulded on a porringer, a velvet dish', the latter term providing a clear indication of its shallowness.

A good many examples of porringers, both in silver and pewter, have survived from the second half of the 17th century and the early 18th century. They almost invariably had a single flat handle, usually pierced, projecting from one side of the rim. An advertisement for lost plate, which appeared in the *London Gazette* in 1679, mentioned '3 Porringers (one with the ear off)'. In the late 17th and early 18th centuries, another variety, often designated by the French word *écuelle*, was made to some slight extent in England. It had two handles and a cover and was sometimes finely decorated. Most surviving examples of this type of porringer were made by immigrant Huguenot silversmiths and it was never anything but rare in England. *See* also Bleeding bowl and Cup, two-handled.

Posset-cup or posset-pot: posset consisted of milk curdled with sweetened spiced wine or ale, and although posset-cups are mentioned in 16th-century lists of plate, we have no idea what type of vessel was meant. It seems likely that the term indicated cups which their owners used primarily to contain posset but which were generally dedicated to other purposes also. In non-academic circles the name is usually applied in modern times to covered two-handled cups of the second half of the 17th century, but this usage is demonstrably unsatisfactory since it quite unwarrantably implies specialisation. A cup of this kind, accompanied by a salver, was later presented to Colerne Church in Wiltshire. The salver is inscribed: 'This salver and cup belonging was presented for the use of the sacrament.' It is evident from this that if the cup in question had been recognised as a special container for posset (or for caudle or pottage), it would not have been considered acceptable for the purpose described. *See* Cup, two-handled.

Pot: an ancient term used in many senses, but especially in relation to handled vessels connected with drinking. Thus tankards and cans or mugs (q.q.v.) might often be referred to as pots, and the term probably disguised the identity of silver tankards before the middle of the 16th century when they are often assumed to have first appeared. Even as late as the early 20th century, the name potman or potboy denoted an individual charged with the duty of collecting cans in a tavern. In medieval documents, a distinction was often drawn between pots and cups which indicated a difference in design, but as the term was generic and had a very wide application, an additional word was sometimes used in the interests of precision. In 1482, for example, there was a reference to 'tanggard pots' of pewter, and it seems probable that this phrase was employed to distinguish them from other vessels such as livery pots (q.v.).

Pounce-box: pounce was a powdered resinous substance rubbed on to writing paper to reduce its absorbency, and silver pounce-boxes often formed part of the equipment of the standish (q.v.) in the 18th century. Though primarily intended for pounce, the same boxes may well have been used to contain sand for drying the ink.

Punch-bowl: *see* Bowl, punch.

Punched work: the chief examples of this technique were found in the late 18th century. At that time, the borders of various objects such as cream-jugs were often punched with rows of hollow beads instead of having them applied in the form of mouldings by soldering. By this means, the border was strengthened and decorated in accordance with the prevailing style, bead-mouldings forming part of the repertoire of contemporary neo-classical ornament.

Puzzle-cup: *see* Wager cup.

Pyx (Latin, *pyxis*, a box): in connection with silver, this denotes a small, covered circular box in which the Reserved Sacrament was kept in England before the Reformation. A 14th-century example in the

Victoria & Albert Museum, London, is engraved with Gothic architectural ornament and was formerly enamelled.

Q

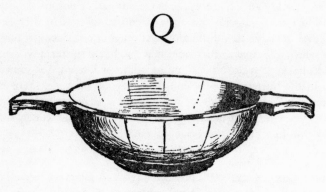

Quaich, c. 1670

Quaich (Gaelic, *cuach*, a cup): an exclusively Scottish drinking vessel which began to be made wholly of silver from about 1660. Originally, it was a kind of mazer (q.v.), being cut out of solid wood, with a shallow bowl and two, or occasionally three, handles or lugs projecting horizontally from the rim, with a short downward extension at the ends. Before the middle of the 17th century they were being built up from small vertical staves like those of a tub and were often mounted in silver. Even those made entirely of silver were frequently engraved with vertical lines to suggest the staves of their wooden predecessors. They varied in diameter from about 6 to 20 cm.

R

Raising: the shaping of hollow vessels from flat sheet silver by means of a raising hammer. The silver is held at an angle against a polished steel stake and hammered down on to its surface, being rotated after each stroke. The stake, which is often shaped like a letter T, is fixed into a section of tree-trunk called a steady block. *See* Annealing.

Reed and tie: border ornament in the form of fine reeds bound with ribbon.

Reeding: raised convex ornament suggestive of reeds laid side by side. Reeding was of classical origin and although used in a minor way in the 17th century, did not attain real importance until after 1800.

Regency style: the historic Regency began in 1811, when George III became incapable of discharging his duties as Head of State through insanity, and ended in 1820 when the old King died and the Regent, George Prince of Wales, ascended the throne as George IV. As a style, however, it began in about 1800 and persisted until after 1830, though the Adam (q.v.) style continued in some degree into the 19th century, so that the two overlapped. Excellent though the Adam style was, it eventually became wearisome in influential circles, so that a reaction was inevitable. The origins of the reaction were to be found in a number of sources, including the work of the architect, Henry Holland, who carried out some alterations at Carlton House at the end of the 18th century. Walpole, commenting on this work in a letter to Lady Ossory, said: 'There is an august simplicity that astonished me. . . . How sick one shall be, after this chaste palace, of Mr Adam's gingerbread and sippets of embroidery.'

The terms used, though undoubtedly extravagant, were evidence of a changing spirit, and this spirit manifested itself more strongly in regard to silver after the publication in 1806 of *Designs for Ornamental Plate*, by the architect, Charles Heathcote Tatham, who had no technical knowledge of the craft of silversmithing. It will be noticed that, in the following quotation from his book, a wholly new and arguable proposition has been slipped in as a mere subordinate clause as though there could be no possible dispute about it. 'Instead of Massiveness, the principal characteristic of good plate, light and insignificant forms have prevailed, to the utter exclusion of all good Ornament whatever.' Although the statement was partly tendentious and partly downright false, the voices of such self-appointed arbiters of taste as Tatham, John Flaxman and Thomas Stothard were heeded. One result was that the silversmith soon became relegated to the position of an artisan who carried out the ideas of professional designers, who were at once more cultured and more arrogant than he was, but who were also quite unfamiliar with the medium in which he worked.

Various kinds of ordinary domestic silver such as tea-pots were, however, usually considered beneath the notice of the new pioneers of fashion, and many such objects were unostentatious and pleasing. But the more important plate, which ought clearly to have represented the highest aesthetic attainment of the age, began to display the quality or appearance of massiveness which Tatham considered so axiomatic, and this soon affected the forms, if not always the weight, of humbler items.

Many pieces such as salts, cruet-frames, tea-pots and so forth, often had bulging sides, while gadrooning was much resorted to as surface ornament. Some decorative motifs were identical with those of the Adam period since both styles were of classical origin. But the Regency style presented a different total aspect because it owed its inspiration to a later, heavier phase of classical art, making use of imperial Roman and even Egyptian elements, or certain Greek designs which had been ignored by the silversmiths of the late 18th century because their ponderous character did not accord with the prevailing taste for lightness and elegance. Extensive use was made of cast figures, including feminine winged Victories or female angels, some of which had a curious flavour of Victorian funerary sculpture. They were executed with consummate skill but were often irrelevant to the design. This was especially apparent in the case of a massive candelabrum made by Joseph Preedy in 1806 for presentation to the future Duke of Wellington. It consisted of a shaft rising from a tall plinth and surmounted, above the branches, by a sergeant's halberd. On a platform above the base of the shaft, two standing military figures appear to be discussing the best means of climbing up it, while two more, seated on the plinth itself, seem to be in a state of exhaustion after having made an unsuccessful attempt. Another huge candelabrum made for the Duke in 1816 by Benjamin Smith, also has figures of soldiers at the base of the shaft. They are beautifully modelled, but as they are very much objects in their own right and are not properly integrated into the design, they give the impression of having been hired to stand about for no particular reason. Both these candelabra (q.v.) provide evidence of the sort of drawing-board design which manifested itself in Regency plate of the more important kind, much to the detriment of its sincerity.

As the period advanced, even minor objects such as sauce-tureens (q.v.) became increasingly cluttered with rich ornament, often of a realistic floral nature, which competed with the underlying forms instead of enhancing them. It is only fair to say, however, that although certain aspects of contemporary taste were unfortunate or even degenerate, workmanship and finish attained unprecedented heights of excellence, so that the period was probably the greatest of all in technical accomplishment in the entire history of the craft.

Apart from the original designs and ornament of the Regency, the styles of previous periods were sometimes used as alternatives. Among these, the rococo (q.v.) style especially recommended itself owing to its plethoric character, and although it carried little conviction when applied to such things as coasters (q.v.) with bulging sides, which had never existed before, many students will sometimes find it necessary to examine the hall marks to resolve any doubts as to period. Other pieces were exact reproductions of earlier objects, including large covered two-handled cups in the style of the first half of the 18th century. On rare occasions, recourse was had even to the Queen-Anne period. The author once possessed a coffee-pot with a tapering cylindrical body, straight spout, and high domed lid covered with small-scale fluting. On stylistic grounds alone it would have been assigned without hesitation to the early years of the 18th century, but the hall marks disclosed that it was of Sterling silver and had, in fact, been made in 1810.

Renaissance (Italian, _Rinascimento_): the rebirth of the classical spirit which, in relation to architecture and applied art, began in Italy about the middle of the 15th century. The Gothic style, which had been imported from northern Europe and never managed to make very deep roots in the soil of Italy, was quickly banished. The renaissance style, deriving with varying degrees of accuracy from classical sources and traditions, began to spread over the whole field of design. It did not reach Britain and Ireland direct, but came in leisurely fashion _via_ the Habsburg empire, which had a common Alpine frontier with Italy. Henry VIII was on terms of warm friendship with the Emperor Maximilian I and England had close mercantile connections with the Netherlandish portion of the Duchy of Burgundy, which was an appanage of the Empire. This was the route by which the renaissance style reached England in the first quarter of the 16th century, and it is therefore scarcely surprising that it should have had a Germanic flavour for over fifty years.

A new repertoire of ornament began to be drawn upon in place of Gothic and included gadroons, flutes, acanthus foliage, classical masks both human and leonine, urns, terminal figures, foliate scrolls and bunches of fruit. Forms also changed as well as ornament. A type of late classical urn with a bulging protuberance at the base was pressed into service as a shape for the bowls of standing cups, while urns and scroll-brackets often formed the stems. Later, architectural balusters, usually inverted, provided frequent inspiration for the same parts.

Towards the end of the 16th century, signs of a reaction against the fulsome German rendering of the style began to appear. A general simplicity supervened, in which ornament was subordinated to form, but renaissance details still remained. This state of affairs persisted through the 17th and 18th centuries, and renaissance elements such as gadroons often accompanied even the novel and positive rococo style.

It is sometimes the practice to include the Adam (q.v.) style of the late 18th century in the renaissance category, but although it derived in a different manner from classicism, it is more convenient to describe it as neo-classical in order to obviate confusion. The force of the original renaissance movement was long since spent and the Adam style owed nothing to it, but drew an entirely fresh inspiration from Herculaneum and Pompeii.

Repoussé work: *see* Embossing.

Rococo style: the word 'rococo' was a French colloquialism of the early 19th century which originally meant extravagant or freakish, and began to be used in this sense in England in about 1830. It was not long, however, before it came to be accepted in France and Britain as the equivalent of *rocaille*, and is now used retrospectively to denote this particular style. Throughout the period of its currency, it was known in Britain and Ireland as the 'modern' style: a term which could obviously not be employed after the style had fallen out of use.

Rococo seems to have been deliberately invented in the early 1720s by a small group of Parisian architects, the chief part being apparently played by Just-Aurèle Meissonnier, who was later appointed goldsmith and furniture-designer to Louis XV. In 1725, the King issued a *lettre de cachet* requiring the Paris goldsmiths to admit Meissonnier to their guild, and this soon resulted in a nation-wide enthusiasm in France for plate in the rococo style. Nothing like it had been seen before in the history of European ornament and, for the first time, symmetry was generally abandoned. The chief ingredients were broken scrolls, formalised rock-work, shells and irregular floral and foliate sprays, all producing a lively and dynamic effect. Here and there, it is possible to detect a faint hint of Chinese influence and even a suggestion of the auricular *kwabornament* introduced in the Netherlands by Adam van Vianen in the previous century; but nothing was copied exactly from either source.

In the 1730s, a second-generation Huguenot silversmith named Paul Lamerie began to make plate in the new manner in London, but it cannot be said to have become widely popular in Britain until after 1740. In that year, the publication of a book of rococo designs by Matthias Lock for craftsmen other than silversmiths no doubt helped to acquaint a wider public with the new style.

A general criticism of rococo is that it tended to produce an excessive emphasis on decoration at the expense of form, and in some instances the criticism is justified. But much of the plate made in Britain and Ireland under its influence was restrained and reposeful, owing to the fact that enough of the surface was left plain to provide relief. A positive advantage that stemmed from its introduction was that so much care was needed in its execution in order to prevent an effect of meaningless chaos, that standards of workmanship were raised.

The 'Gothick' elements that frequently accompanied the style in its application to contemporary furniture were evidently not considered desirable in connection with plate, but Chinoiserie, mingled with rococo details, once more returned to fashion. Though still not convincingly Chinese in character, it was at once better executed and more integrated in the design than the Chinoiserie of the Charles-II period. The latter was chiefly expressed by chasing or engraving, but that of the rococo period was generally embossed.

Rococo fell out of fashion rather suddenly in about 1770, in favour of the neo-classical style associated with the name of Robert Adam (q.v.), but certain minor objects such as cream-jugs were decorated with rococo ornament almost to the end of the 18th century.

In the middle of the century, a new shape, coeval with rococo, was introduced for various kinds of hollowware, and although common enough, was never applied universally. This was a swag-bellied form in which the lower part of the body curved inward, then suddenly swagged downward in a dropsical fashion to the rounded base. It was a disagreeable shape and was found on appropriate objects of all kinds from the largest to the smallest. On casters and cream-jugs it was perhaps less displeasing than on larger pieces.

S

Salad-servers: (*a*) large spring tongs, with flat arms and usually a retaining clip which spanned them, used for serving salad from the late 18th century. (*b*) A large spoon with a somewhat flattened bowl accompanied by a fork in the form of a spoon with prongs cut into the bowl. This type was introduced about 1800. The first variety was probably used for asparagus as well as salad.

Salt, c. 1560   *Salt, c. 1630*

Salt: what is now described as a salt-cellar was in general simply known as a salt up to the 18th century, possibly to avoid the confusion arising from the two distinct origins of the word cellar. One, usually indicating an excavated compartment below ground level, derived from the Latin *cellarium*, a store-room, while the other stemmed from another Latin word *salerium*, meaning a salt-container. The phrase 'salt-cellar' is thus inherently tautological, but it is inconvenient to use the word 'cellar' by itself for obvious reasons. Silver salts were evidently fairly plentiful in the middle ages, but apart from the fact that some were of square, others of circular, section, the absence of survivors from before the late 15th century makes it impossible for us to be certain of the appearance of those of previous periods. The earliest known examples, the style of which persisted without change into the 16th century, were tall in relation to their width and of circular section, narrowing at the centre so that they looked somewhat like hour-glasses. The shallow receptacle for the salt was at the top and was surmounted by a cover

Salt-cellar, c. 1670

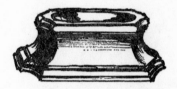

Salt-cellar, c. 1725

which was usually embellished with Gothic architectural details such as crocketed ribs. They varied in size, but a late 15th-century specimen at New College, Oxford, is over 39 cm high and it is possible that some were even larger.

The hour-glass type continued slightly into the renaissance period (q.v.), when it was replaced by a great variety of shapes including, in particular, salts in the form of cylinders or tall rectangular boxes. The sides of the latter might be of embossed and chased silver or, on rare occasions, of painted glass. A popular kind of embossed ornament in the second half of the century comprised bunches of fruit in high relief, often contained in reserves bounded by strapwork bands. These salts were often raised up on claw-and-ball feet, or small cast figures such as classical female sphinxes. The covers were commonly surmounted by statuettes of various kinds including warriors, and the finish of some of these often left much to be desired. Occasionally, the cover was in the form of a fixed canopy, supported on attractive scroll-brackets. This and other types persisted into the 17th century, the covers often being crowned by steeple finials like those on contemporary standing cups. At this period, gilding, which had been almost invariable from the earliest times, practically ceased to be used, but the problem of keeping the white silver clean was eased by a growing simplicity of treatment which affected plate of all kinds. In the first half of the 17th century, a spool-shaped type appeared and was of either square or circular section. The circular variants often had three vertical scrolls on top and the square ones four. These scrolls are often described as being for the support of a napkin, but this is incorrect. A 17th-century documentary reference makes it clear that they were to 'bear up a dish', and they were often shown performing this function in Dutch still-life paintings of the period. This arrangement may have contained the germ of the idea which was later expressed in the dish-ring (q.v.).

Salt-cellar, c. 1730

Salt-cellar, c. 1750

The same design continued after 1660, sometimes embellished with the florid botanical ornament of Dutch origin which was a feature of the Charles-II style, but conceptions were beginning to change. Large, elaborate salts were still made as presentation pieces for ceremonial use, but the domestic salt had entirely lost its medieval significance and people with a taste for ostentation could find many other ways of satisfying it. It was at this period that the modern conception of the small salt-cellar first manifested itself. They began to be made in expandable sets of varying number and could thus be disposed round the table or placed on the several gate-leg tables at which diners often sat in the eating-room. The earliest were plain and utilitarian, with skirt-like sides; they were generally circular and less than 8 cm in diameter, with a shallow recess for the salt. This type, which continued into the second quarter of the 18th century, modified in accordance with prevailing styles, is now usually called a 'trencher salt' for no apparent reason.

Salt-cellar, c. 1780

For two decades from about 1720, a low salt in the form of a shallow bowl on a circular foot enjoyed some popularity; the sides of the bowl were sometimes attractively decorated with applied leafage.

The next type had a round or oval bowl and was mounted on three or four small feet, and never ceased to be made thereafter despite the later introduction of other designs. The majority were plain, but some had lions' masks above the feet and might be richly embossed with flowers. Others were pierced with rococo and Chinoiserie ornament and these naturally had to be fitted with glass liners.

Piercing, mostly in the classical idiom, became widespread in the Adam period and several new shapes appeared. The commonest comprised an oval receptacle with pierced, vertical sides, supported on four feet; another was like a squat standing cup with a circular foot and a rudimentary stem, while the third main type was like a miniature sauce-tureen (q.v.) of the period and had a boat-shaped bowl and an

Salt-cellar, c. 1810

oval foot. All had glass liners, usually blue, which were visible through the piercings and made a pleasant tonal contrast with the white silver. Some of these were made in the early 19th century, but the typical Regency salt-cellar was of rounded rectangular shape with bulging sides. Some were fairly plain, others had everted, cast rims decorated with shells, gadroons etc., and paw feet. They were handsome objects displaying excellent workmanship and devoted attention to detail. The interiors of many were heavily gilded, so that glass liners were unnecessary for the protection of the silver against the destructive action of the salt.

Salver, c. 1690

Salver (Latin, *salvare*, to save): the salver was defined in a dictionary of 1661 as 'a new fashioned peece of wrought plate, broad and flat, with a foot underneath, and is used in giving Beer, or other liquid thing to save the Carpit or Cloathes from drops'.

Silver salvers first began to be made in England shortly after the middle of the 17th century, but were uncommon until after the return of Charles II from exile in 1660, when there was a formidable increase in the manufacture of plate of all kinds. The short trumpet-shaped stem, broadening out to form the foot mentioned in the definition, was grasped by the person serving the drink, the other hand being used to steady the drinking vessel on top. Occasionally, a salver might be accompanied by a covered two-handled cup *en suite*, both being often decorated with embossed ornament except in the centre of the salver, which had to be left plain to support the base of the cup. By the end of the 17th century, salvers had become quite plain apart from a simple moulded, cabled, or gadrooned edge, while the foot, which persisted into the early 18th century, was frequently detachable.

Thereafter, the foot was generally dispensed with altogether and the more familiar later type of salver or waiter, with three or four small feet disposed round the edge, was made in increasing numbers in a large variety of shapes and sizes.

An inventory of the contents of Dunham Massey Hall, dating from the mid-18th century, mentions '2 Mahogany stands to set the silver Tea and Coffee Tables on'. These silver 'tables', which began to become fashionable in the second quarter of the century, were, in fact, enormous salvers or waiters, and special stands were made to support them including a type in the form of a tripod table with flat top and notches in the edge to accommodate the feet of the salver.

Sand-box: a small silver container with a perforated top, used, before the introduction of blotting-paper in the 19th century, to shake sand over wet ink to absorb it. Sand-boxes were often part of the equipment of standishes (inkstands), and it is impossible to distinguish them from pounce-boxes (q.v.).

Sauce-boat: silver sauce-boats appear to have been introduced in the last quarter of the 17th century, at a time when the use of plate was being constantly extended. They were oval in shape and supported either on small feet or a moulded base, the latter being more usual. There was a vertical loop handle on either side and a pouring-lip at each end.

Sauce-boat, c. 1730

This type of double-lipped sauce-boat continued up to the middle of the 18th century, but meanwhile, in the 1720s, a different design appeared and was destined eventually to supersede the first. It had a scroll handle at one end and a pouring-lip at the other and was supported, like the earlier design, on either a base or small feet, the latter arrangement becoming far more frequent. The rim of the body was usually cut into simple decorative shapes, but was sometimes strengthened by an applied moulding which might be gadrooned. The handles

Sauce-boat, c. 1760

varied. One type was in the form of a vertical loop which curved outward from the rim and rejoined the body lower down, the other, known as a flying scroll handle, rose above the rim and terminated in an unattached, inward-curling scroll. Either type might be plain or capped by a conventionalised leaf.

A number of outré designs occurred during the rococo (q.v.) period as might be expected, but the pre-existing simpler variants remained more popular and persisted throughout the remainder of the Georgian period. They were mostly plain, but might sometimes be decorated with rococo ornament in low relief until about 1770, or somewhat later in Ireland.

In the middle of the 18th century, a covered sauce-boat shaped like a miniature soup-tureen was introduced and became widely fashionable during the Adam (q.v.) period, when it assumed the form of a low, wide urn, mounted on a short stem and foot. As the sauce could not be poured out, it was necessary to use a small sauce-ladle like a miniature soup-ladle (*see* Ladle). In the early 19th century, the same principle continued to be applied, but the form became first modified and then

Sauce-tureen, c. 1780

radically altered. The same relationship with contemporary soup-tureens was generally preserved, and many took on a bulging, heavy appearance and tended to display a great deal of ornament including bold gadroons and applied flowers and foliage. These embellishments gave an impression of massiveness in accordance with the taste of the period.

Sauce-ladle: *see* Ladle, sauce.

Sauce-tureen: *see* Sauce-boat.

Saucepan, c. 1720

Saucepan: small silver saucepans have survived from the early years of the 18th century, though it would appear that their incidence began to decline in about 1750. The majority had ogee-shaped bodies and straight, baluster-turned wooden handles, and there seems little doubt that many of them were intended for 'burning' the brandy used in the preparation of punch and other compounds. It is not quite certain, however, to what extent they were used for other purposes. It is difficult to believe that such expensive utensils would often have been relegated to the kitchen for ordinary culinary operations, but a Scottish type, made by itinerant hammermen, was plain and workmanlike and had every appearance of having been made for cooking.

Sconce: a term applied both to a wall-light and the socket of a candlestick.

Shaving basin, bowl or dish: *see* Basin, shaving.

Shaving jug: *see* Jug, shaving.

Sheffield: an assay office was established in Sheffield in 1773 at the same time as Birmingham (q.v.), both towns making common cause before the parliamentary commission appointed to hear their case and the objections of the Goldsmiths' Company of London. The 'Guardians of the standard of wrought plate within the town of Sheffield' were given jurisdiction over a district twenty miles around, their mark being a crown which, from 1780 until well into the reign of Queen Victoria, was sometimes found in the same stamp as the date-letter. All kinds of plate were made, but Sheffield excelled in the production of candlesticks. It is evident that many of these were factored by the London trade, but it also seems probable that purchasers in the capital entertained some suspicions concerning the Sheffield marks. These were sometimes overstruck with London marks and practically obliterated; at other times, when the two sets of marks did not exactly coincide, they were still discernible.

Sheffield plate: this term came into use at a time when the word 'plate' was universally employed in its correct sense to indicate silver, and may well have marked the inception of a modern tendency to use it to denote what should be more accurately described as 'plated ware'. Sheffield plate, which was invented in 1742 by Thomas Boulsover, consisted of copper with silver fused on to its surface. Objects made of this material followed the styles of contemporary silver, which naturally enjoyed greater prestige. Its manufacture declined steeply after the introduction of electro-plating (q.v.).

Shell: apart from its use as a decorative motif, the scallop shell provided the inspiration for the forms of various silver articles. These included shell-shaped boxes for sugar or spices of which examples have survived from the late 16th century and early 17th century. They are generally considered as being intended for spices if the interior is divided into compartments and for sugar if there are no internal partitions. The hinged lids were fashioned in a realistic manner to look like scallop shells with the convex side uppermost. From the second quarter of the 18th century, shell-shaped table-baskets (q.v.), mounted on three feet and with the narrower end curving upward to form a handle, were available as alternatives to the more usual types with swing-handles, but were never numerous. Small dishes of scallop-shell form for butter were made in large numbers from the second quarter of the 18th century and were often supported on three small ball-feet. Owing to its natural beauty, the scallop shell was the type most resorted to, but whelk shells occasionally provided the shape of punch-ladle bowls.

Silver: a metallic element indicated by the symbol Ag, having an atomic weight of 107·9, as compared with 197·3 for gold and 63·6 for copper, and a melting point of 954°C. It is the best conductor of electricity and heat, and is both malleable and ductile: qualities which enable it to be shaped by the hammer and drawn into wire and mouldings. Silver sometimes occurs native, that is, in a metallic state, but is more often found as an ore. It is frequently associated with galena (lead sulphide) and is recovered at comparatively low cost as a by-product of the lead. In ancient times, silver was mined in Britain, but the chief source of supply in the middle ages was Germany. From the first half of the 16th century, vast quantities of silver flowed from the Spanish conquests in America, where a river between Argentina and Uruguay was called the *Rio de la Plata* because Spanish galleons formed convoy in its estuary to transport silver across the Atlantic to Spain.

Toll was repeatedly levied upon them by British pirates, including some with quasi-official status such as Sir Francis Drake (whom a foreign ambassador described as 'the master-thief of the Universe'), and by naval vessels in time of war. During the Commonwealth, Blake seized a Spanish plate fleet which yielded thirty-eight wagon-loads of silver. This was converted into coin, but much of it was melted down later to provide the raw material for wrought plate (*see* Britannia standard). Similar additions to the national treasure occurred in the 18th century, including sixty-three wagon-loads which had been taken from Spanish ships in 1799. When changes in fashion occurred, as from the Gothic style to that of the renaissance, much old plate was melted and re-wrought.

Skewer: it is impossible to determine precisely when silver skewers first began to be used with joints of meat, but it was probably in the late 17th century. Literary references were found in the first half of the 18th century and it may be presumed from their tone that silver skewers were then familiar household articles, despite the rarity of early-18th century survivors. Their function appears to have been the mere embellishment of joints when they left the kitchen, to give them a more succulent appearance, but they could be held to steady the meat while it was being carved. They were all shaped somewhat like the blades of daggers, surmounted by rings or, later, more decorative finials and, until the third quarter of the 18th century, were mostly of thin rectangular section with flat edges. Thereafter, they usually had a medial ridge and were of a shallow diamond section.

Skillet: a small cooking-pot with three or four feet of varying length and a handle. Skillets were sometimes made of silver in the 17th century instead of the more usual bell-metal, and sometimes had an inverted porringer (q.v.) for a lid. Survivors are very rare, but the type is important because it proves that the porringer, which was sometimes used as a bleeding-bowl, was primarily connected with food. *See* Medical silver.

Snarling iron: a roughly ogee-shaped implement of steel with a downward extension at the thicker end which is gripped in the jaws of a vice, the other end curving upward and terminating in a head of varying size. A small, hollow object which is to be embossed is put over the head and in contact with it. When the other end is struck with a hammer, the snarling iron rebounds and embosses the work

Snuff-box: *see* Box, snuff.

Snuffer and stand, c. 1700

Snuffer: this term is widely misunderstood and misused, since many people are under the impression that snuffers were for putting candles out (*see* Extinguisher). Their purpose, in fact, was simply to trim the wick, though confusion may have arisen from the fact that candles were sometimes inadvertently 'snuffed out' while the wick was being trimmed. In the 19th century, wicks began to be made with a tighter thread on one side which caused them to curl over so that the carbon of the burnt portion disintegrated and went up in the flame. But prior to this, the exposed part became longer as the wax or tallow was consumed and was liable to bend suddenly downward and melt a vertical hollow in the candle with attendant risk of fire. Snuffers, which were used after the fashion of scissors, were known at least as early as the first half of the 15th century, but the earliest to survive were made a hundred years later. Some examples from the third quarter of the 17th century are still associated with the oblong silver trays or pans on which they lay when not in use, but it was probably towards the end of the reign of

Charles II that special stands, mounted on stems and feet, were first made to accommodate them as an alternative. These attractive objects, which sometimes had conical extinguishers hooked on to them, were especially fashionable in the early 18th century, but pans appear to have become more popular, probably because it was less trouble to lift the snuffer off a pan than to pull it out of the box-like holder which surmounted a stand.

Snuffers themselves became modified after 1660 and had a box on one arm into which the piece of charred wick was pressed by a plate on the other. With minor changes, this remained the standard design until snuffers ceased to be used. In the late 18th and early 19th centuries, most of them stood on three small feet.

Snuffer-pan or tray: so far as is known, silver pans for snuffers (q.v.) first appeared in about 1660. Some followed the shape of the snuffers and had a curved handle at one end, but the majority were more or less rectangular with moulded edges and with a handle attached to one of the sides. Nearly all were supported on four short feet. They continued in use all through the 18th century and far into the 19th.

Snuffer-stand: from the last quarter of the 17th century until about the end of the first decade of the 18th, stands were provided for snuffers (q.v.) as an alternative to pans. Rising from a foot like that of a candlestick was a short stem, usually in the form of a bold inverted baluster. This was surmounted by a narrow silver box on end, open at the top. The snuffer was enclosed by this almost up to the pivot, with arms projecting above like those of a pair of scissors. A scroll handle was attached to one of the edges of the box and a small socket often occurred on one side so that a conical extinguisher could be hooked on. From about 1690 onwards, the borders of various parts were often embellished with narrow gadroons.

Soap-box: *see* Box, soap.

Solder: the solder used in the manufacture of plate is known as silver solder; it consists of a mixture of silver and copper, sometimes with a small amount of zinc. There are now three main grades called hard, medium and easy, their melting points being respectively 778°C, 765°, and 723°. These decreasing melting points enable further soldering to take place without detriment to what has already been done.

Soup-tureen: *see* Tureen.

Soy and cruet frame, c. 1780

Soy frame: a silver frame comprising a stand with rings in which small silver-mounted glass bottles containing soy and other sauces were supported. They began to be made in the second quarter of the 18th century, the name deriving from that of an Asiatic sauce, imported by the East India Company, which was prepared from the soya bean by fermentation and soaking in salt water. Olive oil was sometimes added, the resultant relish being almost black and often viscous when flour was among the ingredients. Larger bottles for oil and vinegar might occur in the same frame and sauces other than soy, such as chili and anchovy, were normally present as well, the different varieties being distinguished either by labels engraved on the glass, or by miniature silver bottle tickets (q.v.). The stand, which had a central loop-handle on top of a vertical rod, varied in shape. Early examples might be circular or petalled, but later ones were usually in the form of a long oval with a projecting scroll at each end. Nearly all were mounted on three or four feet according to the shape of the platform. Large numbers of soy frames were made in the late 18th century, many having galleries round the edge which were pierced at first and solid later. *See* also Cruet frame.

Spice-box: *see* Box, spice.

Spoon: the Latin name for a spoon was *cochlear*, which derived from the word *cochlea*, meaning a snail, and it is evident that some of the earliest spoons were contrived from shells of various kinds, including those of snails, in many different parts of the world. Even in the reign of Henry VIII in England (1509–1547), a reference occurred to silver-mounted spoons made from 'welke shelles', while later periods have afforded specimens fashioned from horn, agate and other non-metallic substances. Here, however, we are concerned only with spoons made of silver. A comparatively large number has survived from the Roman occupation of Britain, but the great divergence of bowl-shapes indicates that there was no standard form, which in itself suggests that manufacture was not on a commercial scale. The spoons of this early period displayed a number of forms which were to be popular later and included round, pointed and fig-shaped bowls. Though stems also varied in design, some keeping much the same girth for their entire length, while others narrowed suddenly in the upper third, none had any great width and all were comparatively thick. The common Roman device of placing the bowl below the end of the stem, to which it was linked by a short bar at right-angles to both was, though admittedly unusual later, found on the celebrated Coronation Spoon of the British regalia, preserved in the Tower of London, which was made at the beginning of the 13th century.

Silver spoons of greatly varying type occurred in Anglo-Saxon England, but again, the very lack of standardisation suggests that they were treasured individual objects of great rarity. A few surviving examples of 12th-century and 13th-century origin, with vesica-shaped bowls approximating to a certain Roman design, have a general stylistic affinity which may denote that their incidence was becoming greater, for in the presence of a definite fashion we may probably assume a wider production. But long periods which have yielded almost no

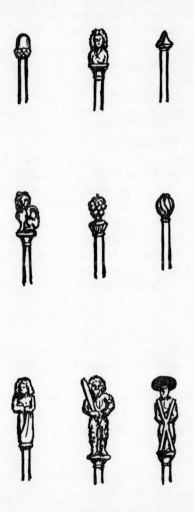

Spoon finials, left to right: Acorn, Maidenhead, Diamond-point, Lion sejant, Fruitlet, Wrythen, Buddha, Wodewose, Apostle

specimens at all make it impossible to erect a satisfactory chronology. It seems probable that the earlier pointed bowl gradually became shorter and rounder, possibly in some degree as an atavistic harking-back to one of the Roman styles, but almost certainly as a positive stylistic development, for many spoons of the first half of the 14th century had almost circular bowls with a lingering suggestion of a point. Even so, the mists do not begin to clear appreciably until we reach the 15th century.

By this time, the normal bowl was fig-shaped like certain Roman and Anglo-Saxon precursors, and this remained the standard form until well into the 17th century. Meanwhile, various decorative finials had begun to appear on the ends of the stems.

One of the earliest was the acorn knop. Documentary evidence of its existence occurred before the middle of the 14th century and it persisted, alongside other types, right through the 15th century and, in a few instances, up to the end of the century following.

Another finial of 14th-century origin is usually known as the maiden-head. It probably began as a bust of the Virgin Mary, for a conventual inventory of the first half of the 15th century referred to it as being in the likeness of *Beatae Mariae*. Thereafter, the religious association waxed and waned. The head-dress often reflected changing secular fashions, and an inventory of the early 16th century mentioned spoons with 'womens heddes & faces'; but the term 'maidenhead' was used as well.

The polygonal diamond-point finial seems to have begun in a modest way in the early 14th century, but had become bolder by 1400. It continued to be used until the early 16th century.

Other finials of greater or less rarity were found in the 15th century and included a cast figure of a seated lion known as a lion sejant, a fruitlet knop comprising a strawberry, grapes etc., a wrythen knop consisting of a spirally-grooved ovoid, an Eastern deity or saint usually called Buddha (though the connection with Gautama is purely con-jectural), and a wild barbaric figure armed with a club and known as a wodewose, which may have represented an elemental spirit of the forests.

The last quarter of the century saw the introduction of apostle-spoons and these were destined to enjoy a long period of popularity. The cast figures forming the finials had a general similarity of appearance but may often be identified by different emblems. Many were surmounted by a disc-like aureole which often looked like a large hat.

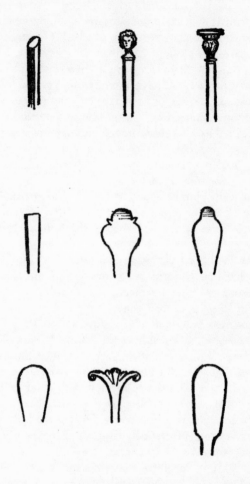

Slip-end, Saracen's head, Seal-top, Puritan, Trifid, Wavy end, Old English, Onslow, Fiddle

The figure of Christ, known as the Master spoon, had the right hand raised in benediction while the left held an orb. St Peter had one or two keys or a fish; St Andrew a diagonal cross; St James the Greater a scallop shell, a pilgrim's staff, or a hat and scrip; St John an eagle, a cup, or a palm-branch; St Bartholomew a large skinning knife; St Philip a staff with cruciform top, some loaves, or a basket of bread; St Thomas a spear, an arrow, or a rule; St Matthew a money-box, a wallet, a T-square, or a hatchet; St Jude a boat, a cross (sometimes inverted), a club, or a carpenter's square; St Simon Zelotes a saw, a fish, or an oar; St Matthias an axe, a spear, or a poleaxe; St James the Less a fuller's bat. St Paul was sometimes substituted for one of the original twelve and may be identified by his sword, though his inclusion is easier to understand than the presence of such secular notables as King Arthur, Alexander, Charlemagne and even Queen Elizabeth I, which occurred occasionally in the 16th century.

In the late 15th century appeared the slip-end, a name given to a stem the top of which appears to have been sliced off at an angle. The latest example seen by the author bore the London hall marks for 1699.

A number of other styles were also known in the 16th century, including a finial in the form of a saracen's head and others, rare for obvious reasons, which bore their owners' arms, or devices which made canting allusions to their names.

Perhaps the most numerous of all normal varieties was the attractive seal-top or seal-head, so called in modern times because the flat knop, wider than the polygonal stem itself, looks somewhat like a seal, though it was not designed for this purpose. From about 1550, it was often mounted on a small baluster ornamented with acanthus foliage. The seal-top remained widely popular into the second quarter of the 17th century after first appearing in the second half of the 15th century. The type has survived in comparatively large numbers and must have been extremely popular over a long period.

It was probably in the 1630s that a change occurred in the bowl, which abandoned the time-honoured fig-shape and became a regular oval. This shape persisted after 1700. At the same time, the stem became of a flat rectangular section and was simply cut off straight at the top. No other type of spoon throughout the entire history of these objects has been so singularly lacking in interest, grace, or beauty, and although it probably had no actual connection with killjoy religious bigots, since it occurred in France at the same time, it is appropriately named the

Puritan spoon. It persisted until slightly after 1660, when it was replaced by a design which remained current until the early 18th century.

This is generally described as having a trifid or trefid end, because the thick, flat stem was broadened at the top by hammering and formed into three lobes by cutting a notch each side of the centre. It was on this type of spoon that the rat-tail first made its début, extending its tapering point more than halfway down the back of the oval bowl. These rat-tails were usually of hollow triangular section and were sometimes embellished with diminishing beads, but they were occasionally of semi-circular section, though this formation was commoner later. Some trifid spoons were quite plain, others were engraved and some were stamped with conventional foliate ornament on the front of the finial and the back of the bowl. The Exeter silversmiths showed a particular devotion to the type and went on making it well into the first quarter of the 18th century.

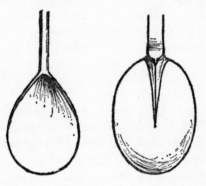

Fig-shaped bowl, c. 1550.   Rat-tail bowl, c. 1680

As usual, there was a general overlapping of styles even in London, and in the last decade of the 17th century a new type appeared and existed alongside the trifid and others. This was the wavy end, sometimes incorrectly described in modern auctioneers' catalogues as 'dog-nosed'. There were no deep notches on the finial forming distinct lobes, the protuberances merging smoothly into each other. The rat-tail also generally changed its character, and justified its name more than the usual earlier variety. It became almost universally of the tapering, semi-circular section which had already occurred very sparsely with the trifid end and, at the same time, the lower part of the stem became more rounded.

These wavy-ended spoons continued to be made beyond the end of the reign of Queen Anne (1702–1714), but in about 1705, another form of stem-treatment was introduced. It became thickened and rounded at the end and often had a pronounced ridge down the centre. This type of finial is sometimes called the Hanoverian pattern, because the end turned up, as in the case of the trifid and wavy end, to distinguish it from a modified version which came on the scene in about 1760 which had the end turned down. The latter is known as the Old English pattern: a term which should, strictly speaking, be applied to both as different species of the same genus. The rat-tail persisted on the backs of many bowls, but at about the same time as the rounded end was introduced, one or two lobes at the point where the stem joined the bowl began to be used as an alternative, so that several variations existed coevally. The author once possessed an example of 1707 with the rounded finial and a single lobe on the bowl, so the type evidently began to be made rather earlier than is generally supposed.

Early in the reign of George II (1727–1760) the rat-tail practically disappeared altogether, and thereafter the spoon with lobed bowl and turned-up, rounded end remained standard until the 1760s, with one rather rare exception.

This was the Onslow pattern, named after Arthur Onslow, Speaker of the House of Commons in the mid-18th century. The stem remained comparatively narrow for most of its length, then suddenly broadened out at the end, which was ribbed and turned downward in a pronounced manner. It was applied to all members of the spoon family including ladles, but was never anything but uncommon.

During the Adam (q.v.) period, the turned-down Old English pattern, sometimes with a faint suggestion of a point, was universal and lasted until the end of the 18th century and beyond. At the same time, the bowl tended to become more pointed so that it assumed the shape of an egg, and sometimes bore stamped ornament on the back which had begun to appear in about 1740. From the 1770s, although many examples were quite plain, spoon-stems were often decorated with small-scale peripheral bead-mouldings, a feathered edge comprising oblique lines, or a threaded edge in which an internal line followed and emphasised the profile.

The familiar fiddle pattern, current throughout the whole of the 19th century, was introduced soon after 1800 after being in existence in France since about the middle of the 18th century and after being known even in Lithuania many years before it came to Britain. Most examples were plain, with nothing but a slight bevelling of the edges, but minor variations occurred before the end of the Regency. The usual fiddle-pattern stem had a rounded finial which remained more or less parallel-sided for some distance and then narrowed suddenly, broadening slightly at the bowl-end to form a pair of short, angular shoulders, the latter having already occurred occasionally in the late 18th century with the Old English pattern. From about 1810, scallop-shell ornament began to occur at the top, on one side or both, and threaded edges were common, but these variants did not compare in elaboration with the King's pattern, in which the finial was covered with surface orna-ment such as scrolls in addition to the shell. This pattern and its derivatives, were more typical of the Victorian period, but all of them developed from the fiddle pattern.

Spoon, basting: the term 'basting spoon' is applied in modern times to any unusually large spoon, though it seems unlikely that such expensive objects would normally have been consigned to the kitchen and the tender mercies of a cook. The earliest example encountered by the author had a long stem with a slip-end and belonged to the end of the 17th century, though examples may have occurred earlier. Before 1700, most spoons of the type in question had large, oval rat-tail bowls and tapering, tubular stems terminating in a domed finial. Later specimens accorded with the prevailing styles which affected contemporary spoons of all kinds and were distinguished only by their size, the tubular stem having disappeared in the reign of George I (1714–1727). As the modern name appears to be lacking in validity, it would be better to describe these monumental spoons simply as large serving spoons. *See* Spoon, hash.

Spoon, caddy: caddy spoons were an innovation of the late 18th century for measuring tea into the pot. These miniature spoons or ladles, often made in one piece from thin silver, were in many designs which included the normal contemporary finials such as the Old English and fiddle patterns and others of a more fanciful nature like jockey-caps and spread-eagles. These last two and certain others have become extremely rare owing to the fact that caddy spoons have, in recent years, attracted the attention of collectors of small silver, despite the difficulty of displaying them satisfactorily. Their ancestors were in the form of small ladles, about the size of sauce-ladles, with slightly pierced bowls, and in the rococo (q.v.) period, were sometimes suspended from the handles of vase-shaped tea-canisters.

Spoon, dessert: dessert spoons began to be made in the late 17th century and always followed contemporary flatware design. They were simply smaller versions of table spoons, but their incidence was appreciably lower, so that they are considerably more rare and consequently difficult to acquire, especially those of earlier periods.

Spoon, gravy: a large silver spoon of the 18th and 19th centuries similar to a serving spoon, but sometimes with a perforated vertical division down the centre of the bowl. Gravy from the meat-dish was strained through this, leaving any solid matter on one side.

Spoon, hash: any large spoon is liable, in modern times, to be called a hash spoon or basting spoon. No doubt these utensils were employed for serving made-up dishes including hash, but as their use was not confined to such concoctions they might be better described as serving spoons. *See* Spoon.

Spoon, strainer: a spoon with a perforated bowl about the same size as a tea-spoon, but with a narrow stem, generally of circular section, terminating in a spike. A few unusually long specimens with larger bowls are known. Such spoons were made for over a hundred years from the late 17th century. For many years, the piercing consisted merely of small, round holes, but became more decorative in the second half of the 18th century. The spike was used to clear the perforations at the base of the spout inside the tea-pot, and the pierced bowl presumably served to remove floating fragments of leaf in the cups.

Spoon, table: table spoons, which began to be made in Britain as specific objects in the late 17th century, were lineal descendants of all spoons made since Anglo-Saxon times. They were designed for any of the comparatively soft foods known in former times as 'spoon meat' and were the earliest soup-spoons, but true specialisation did not occur before the advent of formal table-settings in the 18th century. *See* Spoon.

Spoon, tea: tea-spoons appear to have been first made after 1660 but were rare until the 18th century, nearly all surviving examples, whatever their period, being miniature versions of other contemporary spoons. It seems certain that the same spoons were used for coffee. An unusual type which occurred about 1700 had a twisted stem, other details being normal. Many, throughout the 18th century, had designs stamped on the backs of the bowls. What appear to be tea-spoons with unusually long stems were probably used for eating jelly and custard from narrow dessert glasses.

Spoon-tray: a small silver tray for tea-spoons, which were placed on it after the tea had been stirred, even after saucers came into general use. This piece of plate was used chiefly in the early 18th century and it seems probable, from contemporary illustrations, that it sometimes served otherwise as the cover for a slop-basin.

Spout cup: a name given to a silver two-handled cup equipped with a spout which rose from the base to about the level of the rim; probably used by invalids. Tankards occasionally displayed the same feature.

Stakes: variously-shaped miniature steel anvils, typically in the form of a letter T or Y, fixed into holes in the wooden steady block and used by silversmiths for different kinds of hammer-work. A large stake is often called a bick-iron.

Stamped work: decoration produced by stamping the silver with dies or hammering it from the reverse side into hollow matrices. It was used extensively in the 16th century to make the small-scale ornament on the foot-rings of beakers etc., and again in the 18th century on the upper layer of the more elaborate cut-card work. In Birmingham and Sheffield the method was much used in the late 18th century for producing parts of candlesticks and decorative border-mouldings.

Standing cup: *see* Cup, standing.

Standing mazer: *see* Mazer.

Standish, c. 1740

Standish: the original name for what began to be called an inkstand in the Victorian period. Silver standishes probably first appeared in the late 15th century, for when they received mention shortly after 1500, no further explanation was given and there were no qualifying phrases such as 'new-fashioned' or 'curious', which seems to suggest that their use was well established. George Cavendish, Gentleman Usher to Cardinal Wolsey, recorded that his master 'lost his standysshe of Syluer & gylt' while he was at Compiègne on Henry VIII's business, while in the royal inventory of 1520 reference was made to a 'Standysshe with a lyon theruppon'.

We know nothing of the appearance of these early 16th-century examples and the earliest survivors so far recorded date from 1613 and 1630, the second containing receptacles for pens, an inkpot, a box for wafers and another for sand or pounce. Sand was used for sprinkling over the ink to dry it, while pounce consisted of powdered resin which was rubbed on to unsized paper to prevent undue absorption and spreading. No doubt other standishes of the first half of the 17th century were destroyed in the wholesale melting of plate which took place during the Civil War.

After 1660, several designs were current at the same time. The simplest was in the form of an open tray, almost invariably mounted on small feet, and the various containers were either attached to it or housed in sockets according to their purpose. Another type had a hinged lid which concealed the utensils, while a shallow drawer beneath was provided for pens. This version persisted into the reign of George I (1714–1727). A further variety had a top which was hinged along the centre, one lid covering the containers and the other the pens.

In the early 18th century, the open tray design assumed a more or less standard form which endured for most of the century, modified chiefly by changing fashions in ornament which was seldom lavishly applied. There was a socket for the inkpot at one end and another for the sand-box or pounce-box at the other. The remaining space in the centre might be occupied by a taper-stick (q.v.), a box for small wafers for sealing letters, or a silver bell. The inkpot often had holes round the top in which pens could be placed, though alternative accommodation sometimes consisted of a long, narrow recess in the tray. A pen-drawer sometimes occurred underneath, but examples embodying this feature are uncommon.

From the late 18th century, silver-mounted bottles of cut glass were generally used instead of silver containers. A type of large oblong standish of the early 19th century, with two longitudinal lids working on a common hinge, is sometimes called a Treasury inkstand.

Steeple-cup: a covered standing cup with a finial on the cover shaped like a tall, narrow pyramid or steeple. *See* Cup, standing.

Steeple finial: a pointed finial shaped like a steeple, which occurred from the very end of the 16th century up to the second quarter of the 17th century on the covers of certain standing cups, salts, and occasionally caskets. These finials were usually of triangular section, either of engraved sheet silver or in openwork, but were sometimes four-sided. They were generally supported on short scroll-brackets, one at each angle, but occasionally rested on a collet. The summit was usually surmounted by a turned knob of some kind, or a cast figure such as a woman, a horseman, or a warrior in armour of indeterminate type. After 1660, when the original kind of angular steeple finial was out-moded, a somewhat degenerate descendant was sometimes found on the covers of standing cups, which were themselves declining in incidence. This late variant was of circular section and drawn out of the metal of the cover, into which it merged smoothly at the base. It may have represented a nostalgic attempt at reviving a design-principle which had been current before the interregnum. *See* Cup, standing.

Sterling standard: this implies the presence, in 12 oz (Troy) of metal, of $11\frac{1}{10}$ oz of pure silver, the remainder being copper. *See* Hall-marking.

Stirrup-cup: a footless drinking vessel made of various materials including glass and silver, used for serving liquor to a horseman in the saddle, usually at a hunt. Examples in glass, like ordinary glasses without feet, were made from the early 18th century, but it appears that stirrup-cups did not attract the attention of silversmiths until after 1760. They were conceived on an entirely different principle from the glass versions. Those made before 1800, which are now exceedingly rare, were in the same general style as those which followed, but tended to be hand-wrought instead of cast, as they often were in the Regency. Nearly all, whatever their period of origin, were in the form of a hollow fox's head or hound's head of roughly funnel-shape, the fur being rendered with much realism. Some had ears which projected, but most lay back along the head to avoid awkward excrescences. Specimens of the 18th century usually had deep rims at the open end, which were often engraved with inscriptions relative to coursing or fox-hunting. The majority of surviving specimens date from the early 19th century.

Strainer: it is impossible to say when silver strainers were first used in Britain, but as they were known to the Romans, they may well have existed rather before the earliest recorded references known to the author in the early 16th century. Clearly, such utensils could have been of service in connection with many liquids, including wine which had thrown a heavy deposit, but in the Tudor period they seem to have been used chiefly to strain orange juice. In the late 17th and 18th centuries, they formed an almost essential part of the equipment for brewing punch for, whether limes or lemons were preferred, it was desirable that pips and solid matter should be kept out of the liquor.

One rare late 17th-century type had a single handle, but others were all of much the same design whatever their period. They comprised a shallow circular bowl pierced with small apertures and two handles opposite one another which might be of wire or flat silver with shaped edges, either plain or pierced. Decoration of any kind was uncommon and generally confined to borders. In the second half of the 18th century, strainers were often contained in wine-funnels (q.v.), but nothing is so far known of silver strainers, if any, used in the service of coffee. It is possible that this enduringly popular beverage was always strained through muslin.

Strainer spoon: *see* Spoon, strainer.

Strapwork: ornament in the form of closely-spaced parallel lines arranged in various designs. Interlacing strapwork, probably of Saracenic origin, occurred on English plate of the Anglo-Saxon period and on Celtic objects as well, but the more usual simple versions were chiefly found in the 16th and early 17th centuries. It was usually formed by chasing or engraving.

Strawberry dish: a name of doubtful authenticity applied to a kind of small silver dish somewhat like a large saucer, with low, upward-curving sides. Examples of the 17th century were typically ornamented with punched decoration of a rather perfunctory nature, but those of the early 18th century were often ribbed and with shaped edges. All are now comparatively uncommon.

Sugar-basin or bowl: *see* Bowl, sugar.

Sugar-basket: *see* Basket, sugar.

Sugar-box: *see* Box, sugar.

Sugar-nippers: a name sometimes given to a type of sugar-tongs, which appeared in the first half of the 18th century and persisted until about 1770, shaped like scissors but with ends in the form of shells in which the sugar was gripped. *See* Sugar-tongs.

Sugar-sifter: a small ladle with pierced bowl used for shaking sugar over food. Sugar-sifters do not seem to have been made for the purpose until after the middle of the 18th century, and some examples designated by this name may, in fact, have been for measuring tea into tea-pots before the advent of the caddy-spoon.

Sugar-tongs: *see* Tongs, sugar.

Swage: a steel tool used by silversmiths for shaping work by hammering it on to the silver or hammering the silver on to the swage, the softer metal taking a reverse impression of grooves etc., in the harder. The moulded foot-rings of tankards and mugs were often formed by swaging.

Swags: ornamental festoons in the form of looping flowers, cloth, husks etc. *See* Adam.

Sweetmeat basket: *see* Basket, sweetmeat.

Sweetmeat dish: *see* Dish, sweetmeat.

Sword-hilts: silver was seldom used for the hilts of practical military swords as the metal was too soft to afford adequate protection against heavy cutting weapons, but it began to be employed from the late 17th century in connection with smallswords: light, civilian thrusting weapons which succeeded heavy rapiers as the art of fencing became more highly developed. Few have survived from the 17th century and it is evident that their popularity increased considerably after 1700. Those of the Queen-Anne period were mostly plain and simple, comprising pommel, knuckle-bow, a single short quillon at the back and a double shell guard. The accompanying blade was usually of hollow triangular section, often broadening suddenly at the forte to

Sword-hilt, c. 1710

provide the maximum parrying power. With various modifications, these elements remained standard until the late 18th century. In the rococo (q.v.) period the guards, which might be heart-shaped or consist of double shells, were often elaborately pierced and chased with rococo ornament, trophies of arms, or musical instruments and even the grips were occasionally of solid silver. Many prominent silversmiths made them. Until the Adam (q.v.) period, pommels were generally globular, but thereafter, some were in the form of the ubiquitous urn. Treatment tended to become simpler and the guards were often of a long oval shape. This type continued into the early 19th century when small-swords ceased to be worn as part of male costume.

T

Table: silver tables were of two kinds. (*a*) Orthodox tables with four legs, either made almost entirely of silver, like the example in the Royal Collection presented to William III by the City of London in the late 17th century, or of wood wholly or partly overlaid with sheet silver.

Many of the reign of Charles II were of the latter variety. All types virtually ceased to be made in the first quarter of the 18th century and very few have survived. (*b*) A large silver salver which, in the 18th century, was known as a silver tea or coffee table. Wooden claw tables (tripod tables) sometimes had flat tops with notches at intervals round the edges to accommodate the feet of the salvers placed on them. Surviving documents of the period make it clear that these pieces of furniture were regarded merely as stands, the salvers being described as tables.

Table spoon: *see* Spoon, table.

Tankard: a drinking vessel with a single handle and a lid, usually hinged, made of various materials including silver. In the middle ages, the word 'tankard' was applied to a large covered wooden vessel with a handle, used to carry water from wells and conduits and there was a reference in 1482 to 'tanggard pots' made of pewter. There was always a tendency for pewterers to follow the silversmiths, whose productions naturally enjoyed greater prestige than their own, and it is therefore highly probable that silver 'tanggard pots' existed at the same time or earlier. This supposition is supported by a number of references to 'silver pots' in medieval wills from the 14th century onwards. But unfortunately, the first recorded mention of a silver tankard occurred in the mid-16th century, and since none of undoubted English origin has survived from a previous period, we are compelled to begin our survey of these vessels in about 1550.

The first surviving type manifestly derived its form from that of a long-established earthenware vessel, and had a globular body surmounted by a wide cylindrical neck which widened somewhat at the rim. The hollow S-shaped handle, wrought from two pieces of sheet silver, was of roughly semi-circular section with the flat side outward, and this remained the normal method of construction thereafter.

The lid was in the form of a compressed dome, with a horizontally-flanged edge extending back to the top of the handle to which it was hinged. A cast vertical thumb-piece, known also as the billet or purchase, enabled the lid to be swung backward as required. Apart from a small amount of linear engraving most were quite plain. At the same time, since the large amount of silver required was beyond the resources of many people, considerable numbers of tankards began to be made of non-metallic substances with silver mounts. These included glass, horn, marble, and Chinese porcelain, but the most popular of all consisted of mottled, salt-glazed stoneware from the Rhineland, sometimes known by the jargon name of 'tigerware', though it was never striped or marked in any way suggestive of the skin of a tiger. That the distribution of these silver-mounted tankards was remarkably widespread, may be gathered from the comments of Etienne Perlin, a French priest who visited England in 1558. 'As to the way of life of the English, they are somewhat impolite, for they belch at the table without

Tankard, c. 1550   *Tankard, silver-mounted stoneware, c. 1560*

reserve or shame . . . They consume great quantities of beer and drink it, not out of glasses, but from earthenware pots with handles and lids of silver.'

Such a pronouncement by a temporary visitor postulates a very high incidence indeed. The pots in question are now often called 'jugs', but as it is abundantly clear from Perlin's observations that they were intended primarily for drinking beer, there is no doubt that they would be better described as tankards, in common with similar vessels made of other materials. All had lids and lip-bands, but some were more generously furnished with a silver casing round the pottery handle, a silver foot-ring crimped round the base of the pot, and a silver girdle connected to the foot-ring by vertical straps of silver.

These earthenware tankards remained popular until slightly after 1600, but meanwhile, their counterparts made entirely of silver had been evolving in a different way. In the second half of the 16th century they began to assume a cylindrical shape. Some were very tall and narrow and served as livery pots (q.v.) as well as drinking vessels. The lids were generally in the form of a high dome, often crowned by a small finial. Decoration varied in quantity and kind, sometimes consisting of little apart from engraving typical of the period, but often including embossed work involving lumpy fruit motifs. Many of the shorter varieties, with a capacity of about a pint and used only for drinking, had one or two narrow mouldings in high relief running round the bodies, or a cabled wire near the base embellished at intervals with cast cherubs' heads. Nearly all, in common with other plate of any importance, were gilt all over.

Tankard, c. 1580   *Tankard, c. 1630*

A number of Elizabethan types persisted to some extent into the reign of James I (1603–1625), but an increasing tendency towards plainness manifested itself and gilding became exceptional. In the second quarter of the 17th century, appeared a new design displaying a change in proportion. The body of this type, which lacked a foot-ring, became wider in relation to its height and the front of the lid, which consisted of an almost flat disc of sheet silver, developed a projecting point. This last detail became virtually a standard feature on tankard-lids until the end of the century. The purpose of a foot-ring is to raise the base of a vessel of appropriate type above the table or other surface in order to protect it against wear, denting, or even perforation, and the inconvenience resulting from its absence must have been noticed for, in the next type, which appeared in the 1640s, it was restored in a very pronounced fashion.

These new tankards, while still mostly retaining the pint-capacity of previous specimens, were provided with what is usually known as a skirt-base. This was a wide foot-ring of concave profile which extended far beyond the sides of the body, protecting the bottom of the receptacle and endowing it with an unprecedented degree of stability. At the same time, a low, almost flat-topped dome appeared on the lid, giving

Tankard, c. 1645   *Tankard, c. 1670*

it a form known as 'single-stepped', while the point persisted on the front of the surrounding flange. These tankards were typical of the Commonwealth period and were often fashioned from silver of somewhat thin gauge at a time of political uncertainty when the craft of silversmithing was not in a flourishing state.

After the return of Charles II from exile in 1660, the widespread joyful reaction against the miserable years of Puritan rule showed itself in the abandonment of many restraints. Tankards holding a pint were no longer big enough for the vast majority of drinkers, and from the very beginning of the Restoration period, most of them were made with a capacity of a quart or more. The capacity of a tankard can be increased in one of two chief ways: by increasing either its height or its width. The first alternative results in a loss of stability and, in any event, a tendency to increase the width had already begun in the reign of Charles I (1625–1649). In the period with which we are concerned, therefore, tankards reached their maximum width in relation to their height. Many were plain, but large numbers were decorated in various ways. A few were embellished with simple cut-card work (q.v.) while others were chased or engraved with the Chinoiserie (q.v.) ornament of a somewhat childlike character which occurred on much other plate of the period. The most popular kind of decoration, however, and the most pleasing, was immediately of Dutch origin and took the form of a circuit of vertical acanthus leaves, alternating with plainer palmette leaves, rising from the base of the body above the foot-ring and ending

Tankard, c. 1660

Tankard, c. 1720

at a varying distance below the middle. This ornament was sometimes accompanied by acanthus leaves embossed on the lids, but these were frequently left plain. In about 1670, the rise of the lid above the flange assumed a double-step form, though the upper 'step' was, in fact, merely a low platform with very short, vertical sides. The existing single-step lid overlapped this modified version by many years. At the same time, the thumb-piece was sometimes in the form of a cast silver lion, but this detail was more frequent in the early 18th century.

These broad, cylindrical tankards were typical of the reigns of Charles II and his brother and successor, James II (1685–1689), but mention must be made of another kind which had originated in Scandinavia and after being introduced to Britain shortly before 1660, remained current for about two decades, though it could not be described as popular. This somewhat rare type of tankard was entirely outside English and Scottish traditions, and examples in the original, pure style have been found to bear the marks only of Edinburgh, York, Hull and Newcastle: cities which might be expected to have had some commercial connections with the Baltic region. The bodies of these tankards were almost true cylinders mounted, not on foot-rings, but on sets of three ball-feet which looked like split pomegranates and were attached to the body above by formalised pomegranate leaves. Handles were often double-scrolled. The lids generally had no projecting flange as on normal British types, but consisted of low domes with vertical edges, which corresponded with the moulding round the rim of the body.

Some of them had a vertical row of projecting silver pegs or pins on the inside or, rarely, on the outside of the body, running from top to bottom opposite the handle. Their purpose was described in Grose's 18th-century *Classical Dictionary of the Vulgar Tongue* as follows. 'Pin. In or to a merry pin; almost drunk: an allusion to a sort of tankard, formerly used in the north, having silver pegs or pins set at equal distances from the top to the bottom: by the rules of good fellowship, every person drinking out of one of these tankards, was to swallow the quantity contained between two pins; if he drank more or less, he was to continue drinking till he ended at a pin: by this means persons unaccustomed to measure their draughts were obliged to drink the whole tankard. Hence, when a person was a little elevated with liquor, he was said to have drunk to a merry pin.' It must be remembered, in this connection that tankards were used, not only to provide a sufficiency of beer for one person, but also for sack or spiced wine which was often shared among the company.

The pegs or pins mentioned above were sometimes found on tankards of orthodox type also and continued to occur in the early 18th century, but were found only very rarely after this. The prototypes of the tankards of Scandinavian origin remained popular in Norway, Sweden and Denmark until late in the 19th century, but they do not seem to have been made in Britain after 1700.

In the last decade of the 17th century, large numbers of Huguenot craftsmen, including silversmiths, became established in England and Ireland. They were refugees from the persecutions which followed the revocation of the Edict of Nantes in 1685 by Louis XIV. They made plate of all kinds including tankards, and sometimes conferred a monumental aspect upon them by placing a decorative finial on top of the lid, a device which persisted into the reign of Queen Anne. They were also much given to a restrained and effective form of decoration consisting of small-scale gadrooning round foot-rings and on lids. At the same time, embossed spiral gadroons, alternating with flutes, began to appear round the lower parts of tankards as on other vessels (*see* Cup, two-handled), while an embossed cable-moulding often ran round the body a short distance below the rim. The Huguenots also popularised cut-card work which they executed with great skill, its incidence being highest in the late 17th and early 18th centuries.

In about 1700, a low dome began to replace the flat top on lids which had been fashionable since the second quarter of the 17th century, and this feature continued throughout the 18th century and beyond, despite the appearance of another type of tankard in the second half of the century. The cylindrical bodies had begun to grow subtly narrower in the 1690s and this process continued as a general tendency after 1700 until, by 1760, the narrowness had become very noticeable, the dome on the lid tending to become narrower and taller also.

Tankard, c. 1760   *Tankard, c. 1800*

Meanwhile, early in the reign of Queen Anne (1702–1714), a baluster-shape had been introduced, usually with a narrow encircling moulding applied round the most protuberant part. Cylindrical bodies remained more popular for many years, but in the second half of the 18th century the position was reversed, the more numerous baluster-shaped bodies becoming narrower and more curvaceous and often accompanied by double-scroll handles. Many examples made at Birmingham and Sheffield (q.q.v.) towards the end of the century had bases which were loaded with lead, concealed by a copper plate covered with baize, to give greater stability to vessels which were often lightly made from metal of thin gauge. Most of these, and indeed many others dating after about 1760, were not raised in one piece but were joined with solder in a vertical seam running down the back in line with the handle. This joint can often be rendered visible by breathing on it.

The last quarter of the century saw the extensive manufacture of a kind of tankard which had scarcely been seen before. It was of either cylindrical or cask-shape, often engraved with vertical lines suggestive of barrel-staves, two sets of hoops being sometimes represented by engraved lines or applied bands. The lid was made of flat sheet silver and the hinge consisted of a riveted pin passing through a flange on each side of the handle. These flanges were part of the strip of plate extending backward from the lid. The handle itself was frequently of square section, the lower part either curving away from the body in the usual manner or merging in its outline. There is some evidence that these tankards first appeared in the reign of George II (1727–1760), but there is no doubt that they aroused no sort of enthusiasm until the late 18th century and it cannot be pretended that their design was anything but inferior to that of other varieties. They persisted into the Regency period, when silver tankards were declining in popularity.

Taper-box, c. 1700

Taper-box: a variant of the wax-jack or taper-stand (q.v.), in which the taper was enclosed in a cylindrical box with a handle like that of a miniature tankard and emerged through a hole in the lid. Taper-boxes were probably first made in the last decade of the 17th century.

Taper-stand or wax-jack: these devices for holding flexible, wound tapers for melting sealing-wax probably first appeared late in the reign of Charles II (1660–1685) and existed in several versions which were fairly numerous in the 18th century. In one, two upright bars on small feet were connected by two transverse pieces, the upper of which supported a pan working like scissors and having handles in the form of birds. The taper was wound round a horizontal reel with a guard at each end, the top being gripped by the pan. Another variant had a small nozzle through which the end of the taper projected. A less common type consisted of a central, vertical rod round which the taper coiled upward to the top. These taper-stands were alternatives to the taper-stick (q.v.) and were mostly used in connection with standishes (q.v.).

Taper-stick: a holder for a taper, originating in the late 17th century, in the form of a miniature candlestick in all the successive styles. Taper-sticks were used primarily to furnish a source of flame for melting sealing-wax.

Tazza: the Italian word for a cup. It is sometimes used in English quite reasonably to distinguish certain shallow-bowled standing cups or standing dishes of the 16th century from other types of cup, but in less well-informed circles it is often applied to the earliest kind of salver mounted on a trumpet-shaped foot. This usage is manifestly absurd and betrays ignorance of the meaning of the word.

Tea-caddy: *see* Caddy.

Tea-cup: as part of the general tendency to spread the use of plate over an ever-widening field, tea-cups and saucers began to be made of silver in the late 17th century. Some had two handles, others had none, and the saucers were occasionally in the form of small salvers mounted on low, circular feet. Many were elaborately decorated. The fashion persisted only slightly into the 18th century, as it must have been quickly realised that a material of such high conductivity as silver was inconvenient for containers intended to hold boiling-hot liquid.

Tea-cup holder: a rare piece of early 18th-century plate consisting of a silver saucer with a detachable stand having a ring-top in which a beaker-like porcelain cup was supported. These cups are often considered as having been used for chocolate rather than tea, but the evidence is inconclusive and they were possibly used for both.

Tea-kettle: *see* Kettle.

Tea-pot, c. 1705

Tea-pot: tea began to be drunk in England about the middle of the 17th century. For some time, it was considered to be of therapeutic value and evidently remained something of a novelty until after 1660. The earliest-known silver tea-pot was made in London in 1670 and would be taken for a coffee-pot were it not for an engraved inscription which it bears describing it as 'This silver tea-Pott'. It is of upward-tapering cylindrical form with a conical lid, the hollow handle, set at right-angles to the straight, tubular spout, being made of sheet plate and scrolled like that of a tankard (q.v.). Insulation is provided by a leather binding.

In the last quarter of the century, silver tea-pots assumed a more familiar form which was inspired by Chinese porcelain pots for wine or hot water, tea being made in China by infusion in the tea-cup.

In the early 18th century, tea-drinking became widespread and surviving silver pots from this period are comparatively numerous but much sought-after. They were of two kinds. The earlier and more characteristic was shaped like a pear (pyriform) with a high, domed lid and was of either circular or polygonal section. The handle, which was of wood or occasionally of ivory, was at right-angles to the swan-necked spout or on the opposite side, the latter arrangement being more usual in the reign of George I (1714-1727). In wealthy households they were sometimes accompanied by large silver kettles (q.v.), but were often furnished with their own small stands and lamps, possibly so that the water could be boiled in the pot itself. In a complete garniture of tea-pot, tea-kettle etc., the former sometimes had its own saucer-like stand, mounted on four short feet, repeating the circular or polygonal shape of the pot. These stands, which would naturally tend, in the course of time, to become separated from their accompanying pots, are now extremely rare.

Tea-pot, c. 1710

The other type of tea-pot, which increased in incidence later, is known as bullet-shaped owing to its more or less spherical form and might be of circular or polygonal section, usually the former. Most were quite plain and of small size owing to the high price of tea. Spouts were either straight or swan-necked. In the second quarter of the 18th century, the spherical body was sometimes slightly modified by spaced, vertical indentations, giving it something of the appearance of a melon. A similar form of treatment was destined to be popular in the Victorian period on pots of larger size. Contemporary Irish tea-pots were practically identical in design with those made in England and were of equal merit in all respects, but Scottish silversmiths, who do not appear to have produced silver tea-pots until the end of Queen Anne's reign (1702–1714), went straight to the spherical form and did not meddle with the pear-shape at all. These Scottish bullet tea-pots, which are among the most attractive ever made, differed from their English equivalents in that, instead of being mounted on a foot-ring in direct contact with the base of the body, they were usually supported on a short but distinct stem above the circular foot. A modified version of the bullet-shape existed at the same time. The foot was dispensed with

Tea-pot, swag-bellied, c. 1750

and the body was elongated vertically into the form of a cask. Both types, which were mostly provided with straight spouts, had a noticeably greater capacity than English tea-pots. From the middle of the 18th century, some were made in the swag-bellied form common during the rococo period south of the border and, thereafter, designs tended to approximate to those current in England.

When the rococo style was succeeded by the neo-classical, the swag-bellied tea-pot was followed by several new forms. Fired by the general enthusiasm for classical urns, some English silversmiths attempted to make tea-pots based on this popular form, but the results were never successful. The wide, low type of urn was selected, as in the case of contemporary sauce-tureens (q.v.) and the spout was sometimes made in a single curve to repeat, as far as possible, the shape of the handle. But spouts of this kind always dribbled and, not only was the centre of

Tea-pot, c. 1780

gravity too high, but the capacity was too small for normal require-
ments. More numerous than these were pots with vertical sides and
bodies of oval, circular, rectangular or more elaborate section, the first
being the most popular. Spouts were usually straight but were occasionally swan-necked. Ornament was generally slight and often
comprised no more than bead-mouldings and bright-cut engraving
(q.v.). These pots were often made of metal of thin gauge, particularly
large specimens of the last decade of the 18th century, many being
supplied by Birmingham manufacturers in the form of separate
components known as 'findings', which were bought and assembled by
silversmiths in other centres including London. The style persisted into
the early 19th century and, until the Regency style became fully
established, existed coevally with several new varieties, some of which
appeared in the last years of the 18th century.

Tea-pot, c. 1810

One type was mounted on a short stem and foot, but gained adequate stability from the squat proportions of the body, which kept the centre of gravity low. The recurved spout, broad at the point of attachment, extended the line of the base outward. This, and many other varieties, often had a deep flange extending above the top of the body and, after 1800, many had the lower part embellished with bold vertical gadroons (q.v.) which were normally repeated on the lid and the base of the spout. Many tea-pots in the early 19th century were of rounded oblong-shape and with bulging sides, and were frequently supported on four small, spherical feet to minimise contact with the table or other surface at a time when tea-pot stands were passing out of use. The tops of handles tended to be square instead of round. The capacity of most tea-pots of this period was large compared with that of 18th-century examples.

Tea-spoon: *see* Spoon, tea.

Tea table: a description applied from the early 18th century to a large salver (q.v.) which held the tea equipage.

Tea-tray: quite early in the 18th century, the vessels used in the service of tea began to be stood on large salvers (q.v.) by those who could afford them, and these could be considered as trays in a broad sense, though they were known as 'tables' at the time and later and were usually equipped with feet. Silver trays, in the generally accepted sense of the word, did not appear to any extent until the third quarter of the 18th century, after which they became increasingly common. Some were circular, but the majority were oval, or rectangular to a less degree. Many had a flat base and a low gallery round the edge decorated with pierced ornament in the contemporary idiom (*see* Adam), and an aperture at each end by which the tray was held. A few were made of wood or papier-mâché with a silver gallery, while many others were, of course, in Sheffield plate. The oval shape was almost universal after 1800, but the earlier gallery was generally replaced by a moulded border and loop-handles were soldered to the ends, the whole being usually massive in weight and appearance in accordance with the taste of the Regency (q.v.).

Tea-urn: silver urns for hot water to fill and replenish tea-pots began to become fashionable shortly after the middle of the 18th century when silver kettles were declining somewhat in popular esteem, though they never ceased to be made altogether. The earlier examples of urns in the rococo period were over-elaborate in both form and decoration. In the Adam period, designs became altogether simpler and cleaner, the shape of the classical urn proving eminently suitable and requiring very little adaptation. Most were provided with two vertical loop-handles, which rose above the rim, then curved inward to the base of the body, merging into its outline. Tea-urns of this type continued to be made in the early 19th century, but were soon superseded by wider, squatter versions of the urn, deriving from a later, heavier phase of classical art, and were usually provided with loop-handles attached horizontally instead of vertically. All tea-urns had a tap at the base of the body, and the temperature of the water was maintained by a billet of hot iron which fitted into a vertical socket inside.

Thimble: it is not known precisely when thimbles first began to be made of silver and many are incompletely marked, but there is no doubt that they were more numerous from the late 18th century than ever before. Since design scarcely varied from their inception, one is obliged to base attribution to any given period on such marks as may occur. A great many were gilt inside.

Threading: one or two narrow lines following the borders of various kinds of objects, particularly spoons and forks; chiefly current in the late 18th and early 19th centuries.

Thurible or censer: a container in which incense was burnt, being suspended by chains with which it was swung from side to side. An English silver example of the early 14th century is preserved in the Victoria & Albert Museum, London. The upper stage is in the form of a contemporary building in the Gothic style and looks very like a chapter-house. Censers passed temporarily out of use after the Reformation, but are now often used in Anglican churches that favour a picturesque ritual.

Tigerware: an inappropriate term applied to mottled salt-glazed stoneware from the Rhineland, often mounted in silver or silver gilt in the 16th century in England and used as tankards (q.v.).

Toasted-cheese dish: an oblong covered dish about 30 cm in length, with two handles or, more usually, one baluster-shaped wooden handle fitting into a socket on one of the longer sides. Many had hot-water compartments. Inside the dish was a varying number of small rectangular pans for the cheese, though they are often missing from extant examples, some of which may never have had them. Cheese-warmers of similar shape and size were known in Scotland in the first half of the 18th century, but the majority of surviving toasted-cheese dishes date from the late 18th and early 19th centuries. They were seldom decorated with more than narrow gadrooned borders.

Toasting fork: silver toasting forks were probably first introduced in the late 17th century, but survivors are not common from any period. They were of fixed, folding, or telescopic construction.

Toast-rack: silver toast-racks of varying size have endured from the second half of the 18th century and many more from the 19th century. The first type was of oval shape with wire divisions which were sometimes detachable. This continued until the end of the century, alongside a boat-shaped variety which appeared in about 1790. Toast-racks of the Regency (q.v.) period were mostly oblong and mounted on four small feet. The divisions were occasionally of sheet metal and a central vertical rod was surmounted by the ring-handle.

Toddy ladle: *see* Ladle

Toilet-set or service: various toilet requisites were made of silver in England in the 16th century, but complete garnitures seem to have appeared for the first time after the return of Charles II in 1660 from exile on the Continent, where the King and his adherents had come into contact with a high degree of luxury. Restoration toilet-sets were extensive, though doubtless variable, but few have survived in their original completeness. They included a looking-glass, small salvers on feet, boxes and flasks, brushes, a pincushion, small candlesticks, snuffers and trays, handbells and other items sometimes amounting to almost thirty pieces. Some were in white plate, others were gilt, the skill and artistry evinced in the embossed and other ornament being of an extremely high order. Toilet-sets continued to be fashionable among the wealthy into the second quarter of the 18th century, executed in the less exuberant taste of the period, after which, a lack both of survivors and contemporary references suggests that they had passed out of fashion, to be replaced by silver-mounted glass utensils contained in mahogany chests.

Tongs, asparagus: large scissor-like tongs for serving asparagus, popular during the late 18th and early 19th centuries. *See* also Salad servers.

Tongs, sugar: silver sugar-tongs first appeared at an unknown date in the first quarter of the 18th century, our knowledge of their history being limited by the fact that many were incompletely marked. The earliest, which are now extremely rare, were in the form of miniature fire-tongs and are sometimes to be seen in contemporary paintings. More popular than this type were tongs in the form of scissors, with loop-handles and almost flat ends in which the sugar was gripped. These are sometimes described by the modern term 'sugar-nippers' to distinguish them from other varieties. They continued to be made until the Adam (q.v.) period, together with a modified version fashioned like a stork, the sugar being held in its beak. In about 1770, the more familiar type with sprung arms became practically universal, after having been in existence for just over a decade, the only noticeable change in their appearance being that whereas earlier versions were decoratively pierced, the later ones had solid arms and were seldom ornamented with more than beaded edges and a little bright-cut engraving (q.v.). After 1800 they were mostly plain, and many began to be made to accord with contemporary spoons of the fiddle pattern.

Trafalgar vase: a name sometimes applied to a type of vase or two-handled cup, based on ancient Greek originals, of which Flaxman designed sixty-six for Lloyd's Patriotic Fund (q.v.) in the early 19th century.

Tray: *see* Tea-tray.

Troy weight: the system used in connection with precious metals. As opposed to Avoirdupois, the Troy pound contains 12 ounces instead of 16, though in practice, weights are now always expressed in ounces, however great the number. The Troy ounce, divided into 20 penny-weights, weighs 31·104 grammes as against the 28·352 grammes of the Avoirdupois ounce.

Tumbler cup, c. 1670

Tumbler or tumbler cup: a small beaker with a heavy, rounded base, which resumed an upright position after being knocked and 'tumbling' from side to side. Tumblers probably originated in the first quarter of the 17th century, the earliest reference the author has been able to trace relating to the reign of Charles I (1625–1649). It seems likely that they first formed part of travelling canteens, used on coach journeys, but it is evident that they were later made individually. There was some variation in size, ranging from small vessels suitable for 'dramming' or spirit-drinking, and others large enough for beer. They continued to be made in the 18th century, sometimes decorated with linear engraving, but the majority were plain and all are now rare.

Tureen: two different derivations are given for this word, which denotes a large vessel for serving soup. The more generally accepted links it with the French *terrine*, which suggests that the earliest examples were made of earthenware. The other, which is more romantic if less plausible, connects it with the great 17th-century soldier, the Vicomte de Turenne, who is said, on one occasion, to have used his helmet as a container for soup. Silver tureens were known in England at the beginning of the 18th century and possibly before, but their use became noticeably greater with the passage of time. Until about 1800, they were almost invariably of oval shape and were mounted either on an expansive base or short feet, their decoration according with prevailing styles. In the Adam (q.v.) period, the oval form was preserved but the receptacle was often boat-shaped with a vertical loop-handle at each end, while between the body and the base was a short but definite stem. This type was, of course, based on a wide, low variant of the classical urn. In the early 19th century many tureens were circular instead of oval and had horizontal loop-handles like many other types of contemporary plate.

Two-handled cup: *see* Cup, two-handled.

U

Urn: a late form of classical urn provided a source of inspiration for English silversmiths with the introduction of the renaissance style in the first half of the 16th century. It was of Graeco-Roman origin and is sometimes known as a 'Borghese' urn, its distinguishing feature being a bowl that expanded towards the rim and had a protuberant base which gave it something of the appearance of a thistle. Standing cups were particularly affected and many remained under its influence into the 17th century, but it conditioned the shape of other things as well including ewers (q.v.) while wine-fountains (q.v.) were made in this form even in the early 18th century. Thereafter, large two-handled cups were based on an urn of a different kind, with bowls shaped like a letter

U, but in the neo-classical phase associated with the name of Robert Adam (q.v.) the classical urn became dominant. The Adam type of urn existed in two chief versions, of which one was far more important than the other in connection with silver hollowware. It had an ovoid bowl and a pronounced stem, the foot at the base being circular, square, or polygonal. Those with vertical loop-handles were adapted to form two-handled cups, sugar-vases, tea-caddies, tea-urns etc., and those without conditioned the design of drinking goblets, sugar-baskets and so forth. The other variant was low and wide, and appeared in the guise of soup-tureens, sauce-tureens (q.q.v.), and many other objects. After 1800, taste turned its back upon the slightly feminine elegance of the late 18th century and sought massiveness, and in this new aesthetic climate the thistle-shaped urn returned to favour, finding expression in many items including individual wine-coolers (q.v.). Some of these were of such ponderous aspect that they seemed like reduced versions of the large stone urns in old gardens.

V

Vase: silver vases of various kinds having a purely decorative purpose first appeared to a notable extent after 1660, in the form of the *garniture de cheminée* which stood on the chimney-piece in a wealthy house. It might comprise enormous beakers, large flasks and covered jars deriving their form from Chinese porcelain. There is a modern tendency in some quarters to call the last 'ginger-jars', but there is no conclusive evidence to support this description and it seems unlikely that they were used to contain anything. During the 18th century, receptacles for sugar and tea were sometimes in the form of vases, but they were primarily functional. The same could not be said of some of the larger two-handled cups of urn-shape produced during the Adam period and the Regency (q.v.), the purpose of which must have been entirely ostentatious.

Vinaigrette, c. 1810

Vinaigrette or vinegarette: a small container for aromatic vinegar used to disguise unpleasant odours. Like the word 'epergne', the term 'vinaigrette' is a French-seeming word of English invention. A certain amount of evidence adduced by Sir Charles Jackson seems to suggest that vinaigrettes were known in the late 17th century, but there is no doubt that the vast majority date from the last quarter of the 18th century to the Victorian era. The commonest were in the form of a silver box or locket ranging from about 2 cm to 10 cm in length, but others were shaped like birds, animals, articulated fishes, shells, books, eggs, watches and other things. Most of them were made in Birmingham, where an assay office was established in 1773. A few had pierced outer lids through which the scent percolated. Most had a solid lid to conserve the perfume and a pierced grille inside. The interior and the grille were gilded to prevent the vinegar attacking the silver. It seems evident that they were often carried by men as well as women.

Voider or voyder: a large dish, sometimes of silver, used in the medieval period for collecting broken meats after a meal, largely for charitable distribution. The term was still current in the Georgian period and Chippendale showed designs for what he described as 'Tea-trays or Voiders'; these, however, were made of mahogany and manifestly had two purposes. The only identifiable survivor in silver is a 17th-century replacement of an earlier example and belongs to the Drapers' Company of the City of London, but others still in existence may have been applied to other purposes and are thus not recognized.

W

Wager-cup, c. 1705

Wager cup: in the late 17th century, when English plate was under strong Dutch influence, an unusual type of vessel known as a wager cup was introduced from the Netherlands. An example belonging to the Vintners' Company of London is in the form of a female figure in a full skirt and with her arms raised above her head. In her hands are two scrolling branches between which a small bowl swings freely on trunnions and remains level in whatever position the cup is held. The tradition in the Vintners' Company was that a new member had to drink to the Company from the large bowl formed by the hollow skirt, then reverse the cup and pledge the Master from the small bowl without spilling any liquor. The Dutch were attached to other playful drinking vessels including mill-beakers, but the type of wager cup described was the only sort to find a limited acceptance in England and Ireland. The Victoria & Albert Museum possesses one made in Dublin in 1706. They were never anything but rare as they were freakish and of little use in domestic surroundings, but the type was resuscitated in the reign of George IV (1820–1830). There is no doubt about the date of these as they were fully hall-marked, but many unmarked specimens were made later and these must be regarded as representing a deliberate intention to deceive.

Waiter: *see* Salver.

Wall-sconce: silver wall-sconces, consisting generally of a candle socket or sockets backed by a polished plate, were known in England in the early 16th century and possibly existed before. A reference of 1527 mentions that at Hampton Court 'the plattes that hong on the walles to geve lightes in the chamber ware of syluer & gylt w^t lightes burnyng in them'. Others naturally occurred in the royal residences in the 16th and 17th centuries when they were often called wall candlesticks, but their use did not become widespread until after the Restoration (1660). A few were made in the second quarter of the 18th century, but their popularity did not extend beyond the reign of Queen Anne (1702–1714) and had already waned by the time of the Queen's death. In their heyday, several designs occurred, but the most usual consisted of a more or less oval plate, or one in the shape of a baroque cartouche, with one, or occasionally two, socketed branches attached low down. The central part of the plate, which would normally be behind the flame of the candle, might be either decorated or plain, but the surrounding area was often richly ornamented.

Warming pan: warming pans for heating beds were usually in brass and, later, copper, but silver examples began to be made in England in the early 16th century. Henry VIII owned one and although several existed in the royal household in the second half of the 16th century, it seems evident that even wealthy persons did not regard them as necessary at the time. Destruction in the Civil War may, of course, have accounted for more than is generally suspected. The diarist Samuel Pepys was given one as a New Year's present in 1669 and this seems to suggest that rather more existed at one time than might be supposed from the three sole survivors, one of which, made in 1715, is in the Royal Collection at Buckingham Palace.

Warwick frame: *see* Cruet frame.

Waxjack: *see* Taper-stand.

Wine-cistern: *see* Cistern.

Wine-cooler, c. 1810

Wine-cooler, or ice-pail: silver vessels for keeping bottles of wine cool in iced water were of two main kinds. The first was in the form of a cistern (q.v.), the second, an early version of an ice-pail, capable of holding one bottle only. The latter variety seems to have been introduced in the last decade of the 17th century; most of them, from their inception, contained a removable liner in which the bottle was placed. In early examples, the top of the liner had a broad flange extending outward to the edge of the container and concealing the space between them, but this flange was generally detachable from the late 18th century onwards. Individual wine-coolers were unfashionable in the middle decades of the 18th century, but began to regain their appeal after about 1780. The majority of surviving examples date from the 19th century when their incidence was highest. During the Regency (q.v.) period, they were sometimes in the shape of actual pails but more often in the form of the so-called Borghese urn, with a protuberance at the base of the body to which horizontal or vertical loop-handles were attached.

Wine-fountain: silver wine-fountains were always luxury objects and although they were made for three hundred years from the 15th century, the first quarter of the 18th century, when large sums of money were spent on plate, has yielded only four known examples. These were in the form of elaborate covered urns with protuberant bases and two or four pivoted loop-handles. Glasses were filled from a tap in the lower part of the body. Decoration might consist of simple but plentiful gadrooning or lavish cast and applied work, but the effect was always sumptuous and monumental. An example made in 1708 was no less than 108 cm high, but despite the effect of massiveness, one is never left with the impression that the designs were unsuitable for execution in silver, as opposed to some of the equally massive plate of the Regency. Their incidence probably declined partly because of the increase in the manufacture of flint-glass decanters but, in any event, it is on record that when they were not being used to dispense wine, they sometimes contained water for washing dishes.

Wine-funnel, c. 1790

Wine-funnel: silver funnels for decanting wine probably first appeared about the middle of the 17th century, but were not plentiful for at least another hundred years. Examples most likely to be encountered date from the late 18th and early 19th centuries when they were very common. They existed in two main versions. One was made in one piece with the tube in which it terminated, but was often provided with additional parts which could be set in the top to modify the coarseness of the perforations. This type remained the most popular in the 19th century. The other had a tube which could be detached from the base of the funnel proper. The latter contained an integral perforated plate, but a silver ring holding a muslin filter could be placed inside the base when the tube was removed. When it was replaced, the funnel would not only facilitate decanting but would also exclude sedimentary matter. The end of the tube was always curved so that the stream of wine would run down the inside of the decanter instead of falling vertically and producing foam.

Wine-label: *see* Bottle ticket.

Wine-taster: a shallow silver bowl about 8 cm in diameter with a ring-handle, used by vintners for sampling wine. They were familiar as early as the 14th century, but English examples of any period are now rare and it is probable that none has survived from before the 17th century. That their use was not confined to wine is evident from references in the 17th and 18th centuries to 'dram dishes' and 'brandy tasters'. Sometimes when 'tasters' are mentioned in medieval documents, their weights are given. Some were so heavy that they could not have been ordinary commercial wine-tasters, but were almost certainly cups of assay. These were used by a trusted servant to test his master's liquor as a precaution against poisoning.

Y

York: silversmiths were working in York in the 14th century and probably before. It is known that assaying was carried out at least as early as 1410, but no description of the town mark occurred before 1560, when it was referred to as 'the halfe leopard head and half flowre-de-luyce'. Makers' marks were also obligatory and date-letters were used from about 1560. In 1700, the town mark was changed to a cross bearing five lions passant, but the assay office was closed between 1717 and 1779 and ceased to operate altogether in 1856. All kinds of plate were made in York, tankards and two-handled cups of the 17th century being particularly fine.

SELECTED BIBLIOGRAPHY

Ash, Douglas. *English Silver Drinking Vessels 600–1830*, 1964.

Bradbury, Frederick. *British and Irish Assay Office Marks 1544–1968*, 1968.

Finlay, Ian. *Scottish Gold and Silver Work*, 1956.

Hayward, J. F. *Huguenot Silver in England, 1688–1727*, 1959.

Hughes, Bernard and Therle. *Three Centuries of English Domestic Silver*, 1952.

Jackson, Sir Charles J. *English Goldsmiths and Their Marks*, 1921.

— *An Illustrated History of English Plate*, 1911.

Oman, C. C. *English Domestic Silver*, 1947.

— *English Church Plate*, 1957.

Watts, W. W. *Old English Silver*, 1924.